The Ticino Guide

Gerardo
Brown-Manrique

Princeton
Architectural
Press

ADT

Published by
Princeton Architectural Press
37 East 7th Street
New York, NY 10003
212-995-9620
ISBN 0-910413-46-0

Published in England by
ADT Press
128 Long Acre
London WC2E 9AN England
(ISBN 1-85454-835-2)

Printed and bound in the United States

Production Editor: Elizabeth Short

Special thanks to Sheila Cohen, Clare
Jacobson, Kevin Lippert, Ann Urban,
and Amy Weisser

Library of Congress
Cataloging-in-Publication Data:

Brown-Manrique, Gerardo
    The Ticino guide.

    Bibliography: p.
    Includes index.
    Bibliography: p.
    1. Architecture, Modern—20th cen-
tury—Ticino River Valley (Switzerland
and Italy)—Guide-books. 2. Architecture—Ticino River Valley (Switzerland
and Italy)—Guide-books. I. Title.
NA1349.T52B76   1989   720'.945'2
89–3635
ISBN 0-910413-46-0

CONTENTS

ACKNOWLEDGMENTS

The completion of *The Ticino Guide* is supported by a grant from the Graham Foundation for Advanced Studies in the Fine Arts in Chicago, Illinois. Their generous contribution permitted me to prepare for publication the many materials that I obtained related to this project.

The research of autochthonous and contemporary architectures in the Ticino region was begun throughout 1982–84, while I was teaching at the Miami University European Center in Luxembourg. The main research was conducted in September and October, 1986, while on Faculty Improvement Leave from Miami and acting as Visiting Scholar in Luxembourg; final materials were collected during the summer of 1987.

I would like to thank Hayden B. May, previously chair of architecture and now Dean of Fine Arts, for his enthusiastic support in allowing me to go to Europe to teach for two years in the first place; Robert Zwirn, currently chair of architecture, has been equally supportive. Both have been more than generous in allowing me to pursue this research effort. In Luxembourg, I would especially like to thank Dr. Ivan Lakos, Director of the Miami European Center, as well as the assistant director, Mme. Maisy Dumont, and the housing coordinator, Mme. Elisabeth Prost, for their help and assistance in translating and in seeing that correspondence made it back to me in the US. To my good friend and former student, Jean-Marie (Jim) Clemes, my appreciation for his willingness to accompany me on one of the site visits. From the start, Kevin Lippert has been interested in seeing the results be part of the publication efforts of the Princeton Architectural Press; his encouragement has proven invaluable. Finally, to all the architects who responded to my queries, in some cases immediately, many calling me by telephone in Luxembourg or here. They patiently answered my poorly worded questions in French or Italian, and submitted original materials for this project. Obviously their support and assistance are invaluable. In particular I want to thank:

Antonio Bassi and Giovanni Gherra, Giancarlo Bentivoglio and Guido Brighi, Mario Botta, Mario Campi, Tita Carloni, Paolo Colombo, Rita Mangone and Paolo Monti, Massimo Fortis, Aurelio Galfetti, Ivano Gianola, Vittorio

Gregotti, Rudy Hunziker, Remo Leuzinger, Franco Moro, Antonia Pizzigoni, Bruno Reichlin, Luca Scacchetti, Luigi Snozzi, Martin Wagner, and Cino Zucchi.

I dedicate this book to my wife, Susan R. Ewing. We both appreciate good food and good wine, but more so share a love for good design. Many of the projects, and many of the architects, we have met together. I also dedicate this book to my mother and father, Maria Enriqueta Manrique de Brown and Dr. Gerardo Brown, and to my parents-in-law, Rosemary and Wilbur R. Ewing.

The Ticino Guide is the result of a research project instigated by a curiosity about why so much publicized work of such interesting nature came from Switzerland and Italy. Why was there a similarity in much of the work, though often by architects of different generations? The investigation that followed, first, of simply seeking all written materials of these architects, then, of actually visiting their works, blossomed into a full-fledged research effort that lasted four years.

But the resulting *Guide* is not a catalogue. While a large number of architects are included, a number have been left out, such as Dolf Schnebli and Sergio Crotti. In general, the architects included are natives of the region. The one obvious exception is Martin Wagner, director of the European program of the Southern California Institute of Architects (SCI-ARC) in Vico Morcote. Two of his projects, a two-family house that uses active and passive alternative energy systems and the villa that houses the SCI-ARC program, are found in the *Guide*.

As it is, over one hundred and fifty works form *The Ticino Guide*, the great majority created within the last dozen years. Those older number a handful and form part of the survey for historical comparisons. There are many other interesting projects in the region, often adjacent to those herein. With luck and some courteous inquiry, a visitor can identify their designers.

INTRODUCTION

The Ticino Guide illustrates the diversity of projects built during the last fifteen or twenty years by what is in reality a small group of architects living and practicing in southern Switzerland and northern Italy. The series of Platonic houses by the Swiss Mario Botta are well known, while in Italy Aldo Rossi has commanded attention with his influential writings and increasing number of executed works. Yet the collection of works included here consists of more than Botta's "Casa Rotonda" in Stabio (TI–Ticino canton, Switzerland) or Rossi's secondary school in Broni (PA–Pavia province, Italy).[1] It includes such disparate projects as the new San Gottardo Sud highway rest area in Airolo (TI) by Carloni and Galfetti, the community tennis center in Bellinzona (TI) also by Galfetti, and Massimo Fortis's public square in Nova Milanese (MI). Their architecture is generally classified as Neo-Rationalist or of tendency—the *Tendenza*[2]—and does not follow the post-modern orthodoxy of historicist revival. Instead, their projects result from each architect's conceptual understanding of the traditions of the region. The projects illustrate the conviction that architecture results from construction and the nature of materials used rather than from the application of decorative elements to disguise the structure of the building. Today's architecture in the Ticino bears a clear resemblance to architecture of the neoclassical period. Emil Kaufmann identifies characteristics for neoclassicism that easily apply to today's examples:

[The] autonomy of forms... tied to the demands for the appropriate use of materials...

The wall acquires a vigorous life of its own, becoming the purest reincarnation of its own ends: the delineation of space, its enclosure. At the same time, the new flat roof constitutes only the cover over a space and not, according to some ancient representational spirit, the 'crowning' of a building...

The tendency towards the pure form, 'ideal', towards a rigorously marked outline, the abandonment of all illusionist experiments, corresponding to a desire for architectural veracity, with a search for the pure, original form, with the desire to isolate its parts.[3]

The volumetric qualities of this earlier architecture permeate to the Ticinese examples. There is a preponderance of pure forms, where the decoration, if it exists, tends to result from the play of shadow and light, of wall and openings, overhangs and recesses, which enliven the façades. Even where the architects employ apparent decorative elements, their use is in the most elementary levels, still utilized only to highlight the play of materials or of walls, rather than to hide this. Why the architecture of the Ticino Basin reflects these values is due to the geographical and cultural characteristics of the region.

The Ticino River Basin as an Idea

TI•CI•NO 1. Ancient name Ti•ci•nus. *A river rising in southern Switzerland and flowing 154 miles generally south to the Po in northern Italy. 2. A canton occupying 1,086 square miles in southern Switzerland.*[4]

The Ticino River Basin as a unified region is an invention. If one sees the river as the thread connecting the Alps to the Lombardian plain, then its basin is a convenient umbrella for discussion of recent architectural projects built in the Swiss canton of Ticino and the Italian regions of Lombardy and Piedmont. The projects are informed by the local traditions yet do not illustrate a revivalist form of vernacular construction. At the same time, these projects show clear connections to the best examples of Italian rationalism of the 1930s and to the most refined examples of the "heroic period" of modern architecture.[5]

The variety of work included ranges from single-family houses to schools and other institutional structures. A similarity in many of the selected projects is their design as platonic solids built of common materials which are left exposed to express their intrinsic qualities. These volumes are often perforated so as to augment the discourse between the outside and inside spaces. This dialogue is further reinforced by using contrasting materials according to their functions. For example, highly perforated steel staircases are placed within a very solid concrete or masonry volume to intensify, as in Louis Kahn's architectural vocabulary, the dialogue between their two functions. This is not to imply the existence of a "school" or style, but rather to illustrate very specific concerns apparent in the designs. Three characteristics identified by Kenneth Frampton also explain the general commonalties found in these architectural projects:

1) The relative autonomy of architecture and the need for its re-articulation as a discourse in terms of types and rules for the logical combination of its elements;

2) The socio-cultural importance of existing urban structures and of the role played by monuments in embodying and representing the continuity of public institutions over time; and

3) The fertile resource of historical form as a legacy which is always available for analogical interpretation in terms of the present.[6]

The Ticino River Basin

The Ticino River Basin includes three distinct regions: the area of the high mountain valleys, primarily to the north and east of Lago Maggiore (the area *sopra Ceneri* in Ticino[7]); the urban areas found around the lakes Lugano, Maggiore, and Como, as well as the valley areas of the lower elevations (*sotto Ceneri* in Switzerland, and the Italian pre-Alpine areas such as the Valsassina); and finally, the Lombardian and Piedmontese lowlands and hills, including the plains of the lower Ticino and the Po Rivers.

Cevio (TI): the local church

As with the Po and its other tributaries, the Ticino River has its beginning high in the crystalline massifs of the western Alps. The Ticino begins its precipitous path at an altitude of over 2300 meters above sea level, near the summit of the Grieshorn, and follows the Val Bedretto to the Valle Leventina near Airolo, the southern end of the tunnel through San Gottardo. By now the river's elevation is below 1200 meters, no longer within the alpine region. The valley widens around Ambri (elevation, 988 meters), where it basically runs east-west before it again narrows and carves a path to the lower elevations. Just west of Biasca, the Ticino is joined by the Brenno to form the Riviera between Biasca and Bellinzona, the last narrow gap of the mountain valley leading to the foot of Monte Ceneri. Here the Ticino crosses the Magadino plain at an elevation of about two hundred meters before emptying into Lago Maggiore. There its waters are joined by those of other rivers that feed the lake: the Verzasca along the north shore, the Maggia between Locarno and Ascona, the Toce near the Borromean Islands, and the Tresa which empties Lago Lugano from the east.

The Ticino River continues its journey south, leaving Lago Maggiore at Sesto Calente and forming the border between the Italian regions of Piedmont and Lombardy as it flows to its confluence with the Po just southeast of Pavia. By now the Ticino is a wide river, flowing through a rich agricultural region. The historical significance of the region is clear, for near the shores of the Ticino are found important medieval cities: Novara, Vigevano, Abbiategrasso, Pavia, and, of course, Milan. When it joins the Po, the Ticino becomes part of the major river system in northern Italy. Cities near the waters of the Po include Piacenza, Cremora, Parma, Mantova, and Ferrara. The southern boundary of the basin is formed by the foothills of the Apennines.

Sub-regions of the Ticino Basin and Autochthonous Architecture

The Swiss architects, Luigi Snozzi among others,[8] perceive Monte Ceneri as a physical and psychological barrier dividing the canton Ticino in two. *Sopra Ceneri*, or north of Ceneri Mountain, the area is a provincial environment with Locarno its recreational center and Bellinzona the governmental seat of the canton, physically isolated by the high Alps from German-speaking Switzerland further north. Lugano, the economic and cultural center of Ticino, is located south or *sotto Ceneri*. Lugano and the Mendrisiotto beyond it face towards Milan and its culture, a historical as well as physical reality.

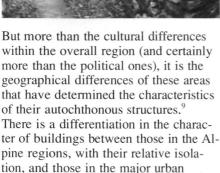

But more than the cultural differences within the overall region (and certainly more than the political ones), it is the geographical differences of these areas that have determined the characteristics of their autochthonous structures.[9] There is a differentiation in the character of buildings between those in the Alpine regions, with their relative isolation, and those in the major urban centers in the plains and lake shores.

The villages of the high mountain valleys in the Swiss Ticino and in the Italian alpine regions are characterized by compact settlement patterns, where structures are closely spaced along narrow paths. Other common traits exist as well. For example, where buildings are placed perpendicular to the slope of the land, separate entrances may be found, each directly from the ground; on the other hand, when the buildings are placed parallel, cantilevered stone slabs are commonly used as stairs to the upper story. The use of materials also varies according to altitude. Where timber is easily found in the upper elevations, stone houses often have projecting wooden balconies to give ac-

Verscio (TI): typical view of a Val Maggia village
Verscio (TI): view of an old town
Bissone (TI): the arcade facing Lago Lugano

cess to the rooms of the upper levels. At lower elevations, the use of wood gives way to an almost exclusive use of native granite for walls, lintels, and roofs. This change in the use of construction materials is apparent, for instance, when travelling south on the N2 superhighway after exiting from the San Gottardo tunnel: above the exit to Ambri, the first type is prevalent, while the opposite is true below. Villages which retain their very traditional character include Corippo and Sonogno in the Val Verzasca. Werner Blaser describes their traditional structures as being "empirically based building[s] developed into an inherently correct architecture" and "primitive architecture which is dateless in its appearance… [and] is archetypical…."[10]

Constructions in the valleys *sotto Ceneri* and in the pre-Alpine zones change in character as available materials change and as the need to protect

Left: *Near Roscio (MI): view of a* cascina; Right: *East of Ossona (NO):* Cascina Malpensa; *and* Bottom: *West of Gorgonzola (TI): a major* cascina

from the harsh mountain climate diminishes. The lower elevations of these zones are more densely populated, particularly along the shores of the lakes. These include Lugano and Como, on lakes of the same names, as well as Lecco (on Lake Como), Verbánia, Stresa and Sesto Calende (on Lake Maggiore), and a host of smaller towns and villages. Bissone—its arcaded main street facing the shore of Lake Lugano—is typical of those in these areas. Their characteristics are no longer those of villages in the higher mountain slopes, but rather of towns benefiting from the Mediterranean climate found at lower elevations. In the center of historic urban areas, more sophisticated uses of materials are apparent. Rather than their structure being left exposed, town houses and public buildings are covered with painted stucco, a painterly tradition indigenous to Ticino as much as to Lombardy.

In the Lombardian and Piedmontese plains, the rural structures present a

contrast to those in the small, isolated villages of the mountain slopes and high valleys. In the lower elevations, the great *cascine* or farm complexes respond to a different scale of agricultural production. The typical complexes include the villas of the land-owning families and their dependents, as well as rustici.[11] These portico-fronted buildings often enclose an archetypical courtyard. Occasionally there are apparently defensive walls, while in other cases there are parallel buildings that partially define a court area. Their architecture varies according to the type and scale of farm organization.

THE ARCHITECTS AND THEIR ARCHITECTURE

That a small number of architects have produced this collection of laudatory work in a region away from the expected centers of modern culture is due in no small part to theoretical investigations which have influenced the practitioners directly or indirectly. To explain this, it is useful to discuss both these theoretical bases and a number of the individual architects themselves.

The Theoretical Foundation

The theoretical bases for the *Tendenza*[12] and for the illustrated projects are *L'architettura della città, La costruzione logica dell'architettura*, and *Il territorio dell'architettura,*[13] among other writings, and many of the historical antecedents for this work are found in the northern Italian regions of Lombardy and Piedmont, in particular around

Milan and Como. However, the largest number of the examples in the Guide are in fact found north of the border, in the Italian-speaking Swiss canton of Ticino, where work of great vitality has been produced by architects who span two generations. In Ticino, this work includes buildings by Mario Campi, Tita Carloni, Aurelio Galfetti, Luigi Snozzi, and Livio Vacchini—architects who began their careers in the late 1950s and early 1960s and who remain at the forefront of the profession in the Ticino; structures by mid-generation architects Mario Botta, Ivano Gianola, and the partnership of Bruno Reichlin and Fabio Reinhart; and works by architects born in the late 1940s and early 1950s, including Bassi-Gherra-Galimberti, Rudy Hunziker, Remo Leuzinger, and others. In northern Italy, projects by Giorgio Grassi, Vittorio Gregotti, and Aldo Rossi of the generation of late 1950s and early 1960s are included, as well as those of the later generations: Mario Cortinovis, Massimo Fortis, Vittorio Introini, the partnerships of Bentivoglio-Brighi, of Caccia-Colombo-Mangone-Monti, and the work of Luca Scacchetti and Cino Zucchi.

It is interesting to note that whatever architectural cohesion exists in the Ticino River Basin is due in part to an on-going intellectual cross-fertilization between the older and younger generations as teachers, mentors, students, and associates. For example, Tita Carloni has served as director of the architecture program in Geneva, Luigi Snozzi teaches in Lausanne, and Aldo Rossi and Giorgio Grassi teach at the Polytechnic in Milan. When Rossi taught at the ETH (Federal Technical Institute) in Zurich, Fabio Reinhart was his assistant; Reinhart now teaches at the State Technical School in Lugano, where the partners Bassi-Gherra-Galimberti were among his students. In terms of their practical training, Mario Botta,

for example, worked in Carloni's studio, and has also participated in projects with Snozzi, among others; a number of younger architects, including Hunziker, Leuzinger, and Ostinelli, later worked in Botta's *atelier*. In Italy, most of the younger generation are graduates of the Polytechnic in Milan. For instance, Massimo Fortis and Danièle Vitale studied with Grassi or Rossi, both worked in Rossi's office, and both are now professors at the Polytechnic. Their own former students and associates comprise the younger generation of Lombardian architects, among them Caccia, Colombo, Monti, Pizzigoni, and others.

The theoretical investigations by Aldo Rossi, Giorgio Grassi, and others of the autochthonous architecture of the region do not illustrate a romantic preoccupation with the picturesque. Rather, the formal analysis of the typology of the built form and the morphology of human settlements is the result of a very clear philosophical perspective. Aldo Rossi established the theoretical underpinnings for the *Tendenza*'s work in his conceptual history of the city, *L'architettura della città*. This was followed by the writings of Giorgio Grassi, including his book, *La costruzione logica dell'architettura*, and a number of essays, among these "Rurale e urbano nell'architettura" and "The licence of obviousness,"[14] which form the basis for his architectural work.

However, it is the seminal work on the Ticino, *La costruzione del territorio nel Cantone Ticino*,[15] by Rossi, Eraldo Consolascio, and Max Bosshard that provides the context for evaluation of the current work in the region. Begun in 1974 by Rossi while he was teaching at the ETH in Zurich, this book provides a systematic investigation of all the villages and cities in the canton. Due to specifics of use, geographical location, and size, building types and groupings show great diversity. Even so, Rossi and his group ably synthesize these into clear groupings: tower houses, double houses, houses two rooms deep, double houses two rooms deep, and houses served by a central hallway; groupings of isolated houses, groupings of row houses, houses with a central courtyard, those grouped to form a large open space within, and those which are transformations of the traditional *palazzo*.

The theoretical direction initiated by the book's publication is apparent, for example, in recent studies completed at the Polytechnic in Milan by Luca Scacchetti and Giancarlo Motta-Antonia Pizzigoni. Scacchetti's still-unpublished research of the built environment in the pre-Alpine area of Valsassina was approached with the same thoroughness as Rossi's own study of the Ticino. Scacchetti catalogues and synthesizes the rich and diverse range of building forms, from pilgrimage chapels and houses to agricultural structures found in the valleys east of Lago di Como above Lecco. In explaining his approach, he states that he seeks to *retrieve a homogeneous architectural language for new constructions in the Lombardian plains and mountains, capable of continuing the traditions of the place and the investigation for a new architecture.* Further, he states: "The characteristics of the Lombard mountains are different to other mountainous zones...."[16]

Thus, through detailed and exhaustive analysis Scacchetti finds a limited number of elements which are utilized repeatedly: walls of masonry or stone, timber for beams, small windows always recessed. A similar analysis was conducted on the urban block and neighborhoods of Milan under Giancarlo Motta and Antonia Pizzigoni.[17] In both cases, the very precise and rigor-ous analysis does not yield imitative responses to the existing context. Clearly, Scacchetti's two houses in Baiedo (CO) resulted from his investigations conducted in the Valsassina area; however, the structures are not revivalist in any manner. While Motta-Pizzigoni's proposals for the Porta Genova area constitute urban design guidelines, the type of rigorous analysis they followed is also evident in their competition project for the community plaza in Nembri (BE). Another exhaustive investigation is one of Pavia, under the direction of Giorgio Grassi.[18]

An Attitude about Autochthonous Architecture

Understanding how traditional structures influence the new architecture of the Ticino Basin is paramount to understanding this work. Luigi Snozzi states that it is normal to be aware of one's surroundings,[19] that one must search for useful values or for those of interest. He sites as examples the precision with which topography and geography are addressed in the traditional constructions, a geometric precision which ties these constructions to the land. As example he discusses the traditional village of Corippo near Locarno, where there are only two building types: what gives diversity to the village is the variation within these types, how they are attached to the ground. This typical attitude investigates the form and content of the antecedents for their conceptual qualities, rather than for the stylistic variations. Aurelio Galfetti expresses similar thoughts; yet, he further states: *restoration, in architecture, is always transformation, because it is true that one restores to conserve but also to respond to new demands, for a new content...[and] in this sense, restoration is an architectural activity, and the restoration project a project of architecture.*[20]

Ambri (TI): view of the town center with the single-family house by Pietro Boschetti in the middle
Vogorno (TI): view along the road that follows the shore of the man-made lake. The hillside town retains—by law—its traditional characteristics. It is in this context that Livio Vacchini built a small vacation house

What is important is that the regional precedents be interpreted analogically, be it the structures in the small and isolated villages *sopra Ceneri*, or the great farm complexes of the Lombardian plain.

There are a number of projects which appear to be flagrantly neo-traditionalist at first sight, such as the small vacation house in Vogorno (TI) by Livio Vacchini, or the three-family house in Baiedo (CO) by Luca Scacchetti. Another example is the single-family house by Pietro Boschetti located in the center of the village of Ambri (TI) high along the Leventina valley, a small structure which transforms the traditional village building while retaining its fundamental characteristics. Its construction is of simple materials: modular brick walls and concrete slab for the lower and main

floors, timber framing for the upper floor and roof, and wood frames for doors and windows. All materials are left exposed. Other projects which may appear to be patently neo-historicist, such as the Del Curto house in Camorino (TI) by Bassi-Gherra-Galimberti or the apartment block in Seriate (BE) by Mario Cortinovis, are clearly not so. What distinguishes these projects from others truly neo-traditionalist or neo-historicist in nature is that they have transcended beyond simple imitation to the transformation of the conceptual characteristics of the antecedents.

THE GENERATION OF THE 1950S

The Architects in Ticino

In their early work, Ticinese architects Carloni, Galfetti, Snozzi, and Vacchini demonstrate a predilection for the masters of the modern movement. Tita Carloni's work of the 1950s pays homage to the prairie style of Frank Lloyd Wright. Aurelio Galfetti's early work is clearly brutalist in the tradition of Le Corbusier. Luigi Snozzi and Livio Vacchini reflect an affinity for the purist aesthetic of an early Corbusier, Oud, or Stam.

While these four Ticinese architects maintain individual practices, they have at times joined forces with each other in different mixes, and, in fact, Snozzi and Vacchini practiced in partnership early in their careers. The four are joined by contemporaries

Mario Campi and Franco Pessina, as well as the younger Mario Botta. Certainly, the most important Ticinese projects of the last two decades are by these architects.

Tita Carloni began his career designing very fine prairie-school revival houses, such as those in Arosio (TI) and Ligornetto (TI). Of this period he states:

We naively set ourselves the objective of an 'organic' Ticino, in which the values of modern culture were to be interwoven in a natural way with our local tradition.[21]

After a number of years serving as director of the school in Geneva, he has returned to active practice. With Julia Carloni he recently completed his own house in Rovio. This new structure clearly reveals his understanding of the fundamental characteristics of the constructive traditions of the Ticino. He illustrates these traditions in a discussion of three nearby chapels, each from a different century. While the exteriors of the three result from a construction technique clearly in line with the most traditional and mundane of local structures, there is a surreal contrast afforded by the decorative detail of the interior. Nowhere is this clearer than in the Baroque chapel north of Rovio. It is a stone rubble construction, with very provincial pilasters and other external elements. But the quality of the frescoes within the chapel demonstrates the skill and sophistication of the artisans and artists

Rovio (TI): exterior view of the 17th century chapel. The simple detailing testifies to its provincial origins
Interior view of the 17th century chapel. In contrast to the exterior, the interior of the structure is highly ornamented, attesting to the elevated level of artistry in the region
Chapel of S. Vigilio (12th century). Albeit constructed in a very rudimentary fashion, the chapel still contains the essential elements of Romanesque architecture

of the region. This very contrast, between a less refined exterior and an exquisite interior, characterizes the new Carloni house and is a quality also found in numerous buildings by others, including Carloni's former assistant, Mario Botta. While writing about

Botta, Carloni, in a certain way, is interpreting his own architecture:

Mario Botta's constructional revolution has other roots, substantially. One is certainly to be found in the silent lessons of peasant architecture in the pre-Alpine valleys and the Po valley, based essentially on the solid wall (of stone or brick) and great covered voids (porticoes, lofts, the great threshing hearths) where protection is the aim rather than enclosure. Another source lies in the Romanesque—mainly Lombard—architecture, in which the compact wall alone defines the cavity, and there are unambiguous and precise points of perforation…while coverings in the sense of additional layer… are almost completely absent. A third source is to be found in the Kahnian break-down of the various 'containers' of space into successive phases.[22]

While Aurelio Galfetti's early work exhibits the influence of Le Corbusier's brutalist architecture, his current work is primarily concerned with the collective memory of Bellinzona, a city between two walls. The resulting architecture is clearly not historicist; Galfetti's use of the traditions and elements of the region is more concerned with a fundamental, conceptual understanding than with replication or even allusion to the traditions of the Ticino. To Galfetti, tradition is "how one lived in the past;"[23] to use forms related to any other period of history than the present is to work outside of the context, an attitude which gains importance as one works closer to the city, where the traditions and forms are stronger. For example, he questions building modern vacation homes in the rural areas using the materials and form of the traditional *rustici*, since these rural structures are indelibly tied to the land, a building form integral to the agricultural needs and construction skills of those who developed it rather than to our present

Bellinzona (TI): Centro tennistico comunale. View between the walls

needs. For Aurelio Galfetti, it is heretical to use history in such banal ways.

Instead, Galfetti alludes to Bellinzona's physiognomy by using the double wall as a major theme in his architecture: in the new post office building, parallel planes enclose the support functions to the main hall; parallel walls form the primary structure of the new tennis center; the urban villas are organized with parallel thick walls. Also recurring in his work is the use of horizontal bands, from those created by material changes (which he uses in the post office) to those resulting from the peculiarities of casting a concrete wall *in situ* (found in the tennis center or the urban villas). In either of these cases, the bands result from tectonic explorations on the use of materials and construction techniques, beyond simple appliqué of color changes onto the surface of walls.

In Aurelio Galfetti's vision, a pattern of insertions into the fabric of Bellinzona—particularly in the late nineteenth-century neighborhoods—

Brione/Minusio (TI): Casa Kalmann. A more typical vacation house appears in the background

will establish a new order for the city. This visionary plan incorporates the major incursions by Galfetti to date, beginning with the public swimming complex done in association with Flora Ruchat and Ivo Trümpy in 1967–70. The complex forms the spine of the public recreation area connecting the city to the river. Included are the new tennis club, the existing soccer/football stadium, ice skating rink, and proposed indoor pool to the north of the public pools. Galfetti further proposes new multi-family housing to the south. This new housing would be located on sites to the north and east of the existing public schools complex. Thus the density would be increased in this under-developed area of the city, while to the north of the recreational area, a district of single-family houses would remain.

As with Carloni's early work, the influence of prairie style architecture is evident in the earliest work of Luigi Snozzi, the Lucchini house in Faido (TI) of 1958–59. Although the building, with its rubble wall base and upper sections in wood, reflects the alpine architecture of the area, the heavy stone planes defining the spaces within the house are clearly removed from the traditional house forms found in even the upper elevations. Clearly, this is a regional reinterpretation of Wright's organic architecture. However, Snozzi's later work, in particular the social housing in Locarno and the multi-use building in Carasso, both designed with Livio Vacchini, is more akin to Mies's architecture from the Chicago period.

The Modern Movement, seen in a critical context, represents a crucial reference point for my work, and the great emotional response that certain buildings have elicited—and still elicit—in me have certainly influenced my mode of expression. Rather than searching for a style I am concerned with a search for formal reduction: against the loud formal din of postmodernism I propose highly restrained silence.[24]

The architecture of Luigi Snozzi, particularly his villas, responds to a very specific notion of how architectural space is arranged and what is the spatial experience. The demarcation of the path forms the prevalent schema in his work: there is a gate which leads to a bridge which ends in the primary space. This arrangement is found in projects spanning the breadth of his practice, from the Cavalli house in Verscio (TI), where the procession occurs in the exterior, to the gymnasium in Monte Carasso (TI), where the transition is internal.

The work of the partnership of Mario Campi and Franco Pessina, which included Niki Piazzoli from 1969 to 1983, is marked by a clear definition of elements in terms of the whole. Whether it is the conversion of an existing and historic structure, as with the new museum in the Castello Montebello of Bellinzona, or the design of a free-standing house sited among nondescript contemporaries, as is the case with their various projects in the vicinity of Lugano, the nature of the volume and the articulation of its façades is clearly a compositional exercise of primary solids and consistent use of materials. The gymnasium in Neggio, for instance, is a pure concrete

Bellinzona (TI): Castello di Montebello. Campi-Pessina-Piazzoli have inserted a new structure within the old. The intervention is not allowed to touch the historic elements, as is visible in the platform leading into the museum.

Arosio (TI): view toward the upper town. The small structure in the foreground houses a transformer and is constructed to mimic the traditional constructions. In the backgound, the Casa Maggi by Campi-Pessina-Piazzoli

rectangle with a front façade perforated by progressively smaller voids. The cylinder housing the stair in the gymnasium is visible through the perforations. Contrasting materials are used to differentiate the nature of their function, from the cast-in-place concrete supporting walls to the steel beams of the roof structure of the gymnasium. In the Maggi house in Arosio, the concern of Campi-Pessina-Piazzoli is with the definition of the house proper, vis-a-vis

the false temple front facing the town. Within their most recent work, there is an affinity to the spiritual precursors of the present generation. One can see clear relationships between the façades of the Polloni house in Origlio, or the row houses in Massagno, for example, to Terragni's Casa del Fascio in Como.[25]

The influences found in the work of Campi-Pessina(-Piazzoli) are varied. As with other Ticinese architects of their generation, Campi and Pessina looked to the outside for inspiration. Mario Campi writes:

At first our work was strongly characterized by the prevailing sense of experimentation in the 1950s and 1960s, when the influence of Frank Lloyd Wright, Louis Kahn and Le Corbusier was strongly felt in the Ticino. But slowly, as our buildings began to rise, and then abandon us, we turned our attention to a certain type of Italian Rationalism, particularly that of Como and Milan... our focus on a particular historical experience came to coincide with regional and geographical limits.[26]

He gives a more telling explanation for turning away from influences from afar to those culturally in their backyard:

The Rationalist language still possesses its own sense of ethics, internal to the architecture, a morality of construction that ties us not only to the Rationalist experience, but to the artisanal and professional traditions shared by other Ticinese, Domenico Fontana, Francesco Borromini, and Carlo Maderno, among them.[27]

The Lombardian Architects

Among the architects of northern Italy, Vittorio Gregotti is the practitioner with a large body of work not only in Lombardy and Piedmont but also elsewhere in Italy and around the world, while Aldo Rossi is the architect/theoretician who paves the way for a

*Módena (MO): Cemetery of S. Cataldo.
View of the Jewish cemetery with the
addition in the background*

new architecture based on the understanding of the fundamental elements
of architecture, an exploration of the nature of architecture devoid of any socio-
cultural or stylistic trappings.

Slightly older than the others in this
group, Vittorio Gregotti began his
career in 1951. His early work is rather
tentative and shows the influence of his
mentor, Ernesto Rogers. Gregotti begins to explore the notions of type as a
formal element with the 1968 competition for the ZEN housing estate in
Palermo.[28] This is evident in the later
project for the headquarters of the G.G.
Feltrinelli Foundation in Milan. Here,
Gregotti recognizes and transforms the
many and varied historical elements
found on the site. A new intervention
emerges free from historicist references
but clearly influenced by their typology.[29]

The significance of Aldo Rossi is
due equally to his theoretical writings
and to his built projects. While great attention has been paid to *L'architettura
della città*, his buildings are the laboratories for experimentation and the exposition of his writings. Rossi explores
compositions based on archetypal elements. From the city hall square in
Segrate (MI) and the Gallaratese 2
apartment building in Milan to the San
Cataldo cemetery under construction in
Módena, the organization is one of
pure elements arranged according to
simple rules based on the analogical

transformation of established building
types. Rossi's projects, regardless of
scale, are based on "inventory and
memory."[30] About the Gallaratese
project, Michael Mostoller writes:

*Rossi achieves this poetry of form
beyond speech: poetry derived not only
from metaphor and analogy, but from
repetition. The power of Rossi's eccen-
tric, surreal, personal architecture is the
endless repetition and variation of the
thing and its essence. The Gallaratese
seems as if it has always been there.[31]*

The work of Aldo Rossi has become
progressively more involved, as seen in
the apartment building on Rauchstrasse
in Berlin, or in the recently completed
office building in Turin. But these
remain essentially simple structures
resolving specific programmatic requirements through the use of archetypal elements, "familiar objects
whose form and position are already
fixed but whose meanings may be
changed, whose common emotional ap-
peal reveals timeless concerns."[32]

THE SECOND GENERATION AND THE REALITY OF PRACTICE

Ticino

The realities of architectural practice
are such that proposals of great merit
often are not built, and that long
periods of time pass before works are
realized. This is the case regardless of
location. In Switzerland, however, architects such as Mario Botta and others
have been able to see realized a vast
majority of their proposals, due in no
small part to the felicitous growth experienced in the Canton. This has
resulted primarily in commissions for
detached, single family structures—and
thus the preponderance of Swiss examples of this building type in the
Guide. In general, the work by the
younger generation indicates diverse attitudes about the traditions of the

region, similar to the variety of attitudes of the older architects.

Mario Botta has been the subject of much attention since the publication of one of his earliest works, the parish house in Genestrerio. This project was built in 1961–63 while he was still an art student in Milan, prior to attending architecture school in Venice. It is well known that Botta counts as his most important influences Carlo Scarpa, Le Corbusier, and Louis Kahn. Mario Botta studied with Scarpa in Venice, and he worked briefly with Le Corbusier in 1965 on a proposed hospital and with Louis Kahn in 1969 on the design for a congress center, both for Venice. But the formative influences are clearly from the Ticino, both the cultural context and the immediate experiences of Botta. This is seen in the illustrated projects. Botta worked in Tita Carloni's studio prior to the beginning of his education; from Carloni he learned the need for contemporary trends in architectural design to result from an understanding of the local traditions of construction without replicating these traditions. Botta states,

I do believe that good quality can only be achieved through dialectic confrontation; a way to respect the environment whether natural or human—that is transformed by men—is that of challenging it, of setting a dialectic relationship with it so that what is old and what is new stand out by contrast.[33]

Mario Botta's architecture is marked by its clarity in form and execution. There are no unclear relationships. Construction is in masonry or stone; typically symmetrical, the volumes are carved to reveal the interiors, and their central axis is accentuated by a roof element—a vaulted or pyramidal skylight. Botta relies on the Romanesque notion of construction ("an essential, primary style able to create spaces by means of very few materials"[34]). An important

Stabio (TI): Mario Botta's "Villa Rotonda" in its setting

aspect of Mario Botta's practice is his role as mentor. Just as he apprenticed in Carloni's studio, so have a number of the younger generation of architects apprenticed in Botta's own studio. Elio Ostinelli was there in the early 1970s, as were Emilio Bernegger and Rudy Hunziker. By the late 1970s, Remo Leuzinger had joined the group of assistants. Each went on to establish his own studio, and their work reveals Botta's influence.

The evolution of Ivano Gianola as an architect presents a contrast to convention. A very talented designer, he forwent formal architectural training and instead apprenticed with a building design firm in Zurich before beginning his "autodidactic" professional activity which included stints with Snozzi, Botta, and others. Because of his interest in the process of building and on how to detail elements of construction, Gianola's work reminds some critics of the pre-war work of German architect Heinrich Tessenov. This facility that Gianola demonstrates for approaching even the most minute design problems with an eye to innovation in construction has resulted in a diversity of projects that cannot be easily classified. They vary from very sensitive minor renovations of existing structures, where the concern is for the modernization and normalization of the structure, to the reinterpretation of specific tendencies in modern architecture while designing new constructions. The

Balerna (TI): community cemetery. The entrance structures and appended chapels are constructed with alternating bands of light and dark stone
Morbio Superiore (TI): house. In the process of restoring this house, Ivano Gianola uncovered and subsequently renovated the painted alternating bands that animate the façade
Coldrerio (TI): "Casa Tognano."

first is illustrated by the renovation of his own house in Morbio Superiore (1976), done so as to not distort the original character of the building. Gianola is credited with rediscovering the use of horizontal stripes or bands on the façade when he restored his house to its original condition. The second type of approach is apparent in the house in Cugnasco, which makes clear allusion to Le Corbusier's work of the 1950s, such as the Maisons Jaoul outside Paris. An earlier project by Gianola makes similar allusions. In the maternity school in Balerna (1971–74), the organization and sectional characteristics are based on the Venice hospital proposal that Corbusier prepared in 1965.

His recent restoration and additions to a complex in Coldrerio bring together all of Gianola's skills as a designer. The main structures of the Casa Tognano are converted into guest rooms, meeting rooms, and design studios. New constructions include a highly original swimming basin. The restoration involved not only accommodating the new functions within the old structure, but also forming an environment that will foment creative activities. Gianola's details are exquisite—joints are cleverly articulated, wood receives a light varnish to allow its own color to show through, windows are held open by counterweights—and he benefits from using the same craftsmen and cabinet makers in all his projects. The results are not so much indications of a formal investigation as of an understanding of the craft of building.

Paolo Moro began his architectural career as apprentice in Luigi Snozzi and Livio Vacchini's studios in the late 1960s and early 1970s, after studies at the State Technical School (S.T.S.) in Lugano. Franco Moro studied at the S.T.S. and the University of Geneva.

Gresso (TI): view of the village. In the foreground, the vacation house by Paolo and Franco Moro

The brothers opened their professional office in 1978, though their professional activity began nine years before. From the beginning, the projects of the Moro brothers have indicated a sensitivity to the inherent qualities of the autochthonous architecture of the Ticino. Their very first project, a vacation house in the remote village of Gresso (1969), shows a clear understanding of the relationship of building to the site and of the traditional forms. The subsequent residences designed by the Moro brothers illustrate a transformation of this, evolving to the much more abstract building in Porza, with its trussed front façade along the diagonal of a cube. What is consistent in these projects is a concern for clarity in massing and a dialogue between inside and outside intensified by the use of contrasting materials.

Rudy Hunziker's independent professional activity began in 1979, the year when he completed his house and studio in Tesserete. He attended the S.T.S. in Lugano and, upon completion of his studies in 1972, joined the office of Mario Botta, where he was involved in the design of numerous projects including the secondary school in Morbio Inferiore and the library of the Capuchin monastery in Lugano. Hunziker's own work shows the influence of these early years, but more importantly it reflects his own investigations of "place" in architecture: how the environment and culture affect new constructions. Of Hunziker's work, Alberto Sartoris writes:

His work is a quest for fullness in view of the logical realization of programs that lead to their own blossoming. The architecture offers itself in the pure simplicity of non figurative aspects that have not been assumed as a system.

Rudy Hunziker's architecture also shows effectively that it is a vehicle of knowledge. It accepts, according to critical modes, the confrontation with the innovations that surround, enrich and absorb it. Hunziker's work is located on a trajectory whose distinguishing marks enable it to be counted among the demonstrative performances of the art of building of the present time.[35]

Hunziker's role as architect is augmented by that of teacher. Since 1980, he has taught part-time in the United States.[36] In this way, he continues his investigations while also expanding his own perspectives. As a result, his work now shows a maturing transformation from its earlier figuration. The project for housing in Denmark, his first intervention outside of Switzerland and soon to be under construction, will serve as a barometer of this growth.

Lombardy

A different situation exists in Italy. Cities are much larger, and a greater percentage of the population lives in denser conditions than in Switzerland. As a result, there are many more multi-family structures being built than fine examples of single-family houses, together with a wide range of other building types, from community facilities to industrial structures. These are illustrated as well. But the Italian condition diverges from what is found north of the border in other ways. The study of a number of proposals in Lombardy is the key to fully understanding the impact and influence of the autochthonous architecture found in the Basin, particularly since among the important architects are those who have yet to build. Specifically one finds Danièle Vitale, Giancarlo Motta, and Antonia Pizzigoni in this category. They are among those whose development is tied to the teachings of Aldo Rossi. Another characteristic of those practicing in Lombardy is their close connection. All are products of the Polytechnic of Milan, now teach there, and form part of the Rossi/Grassi circle.

Born in Muralto, Ticino, Danièle Vitale received his education and began his professional development in Milan, where he both studied under and worked with Rossi. His professional career has been one of investigation, including the 1974–76 analysis of the Porta Ticinese area of Milan, a project directed with Massimo Fortis and Giancarlo Motta, and an investigation on the "architectural project and its relation to antiquity and tradition," with Giorgio Grassi. He is, as well, one of the more influential writers and critics of the contemporary scene. Vitale's most relevant recent projects are the competition project of 1984 for the Porto Navile park in Bologna and the 1986 competition entry for the redevelopment of the area around S. Lorenzo in Milan. Both projects clearly result from a similar set of concerns for the typology of the structures and the morphology of the urban area.

Massimo Fortis lives a professional life divided between academia and architectural practice, characterized by an attitude of cooperative interchange. He was a student at the Polytechnic in Milan, finished his professional studies with Aldo Rossi and Giorgio Grassi, with whom he collaborated from 1970 to 1972, and has taught architectural composition at his *alma mater* since

1974. Fortis has designed numerous residential, educational, and recreational facilities. All are realizations of his design philosophy:

I believe in architecture as an objective art where individual skills elaborate those aesthetic concepts which belong to the collective consciousness of history and of the city.[37]

The first project by Massimo Fortis was the renovation and extension to the national boarding school in Novara, done in association with his engineer father, Federico Fortis. The intervention is in a context of disparate structures which Fortis ties together with new constructions. While the overall solution may appear disjointed, there is an overall concept:

My view of design can be called a mildly mannerist form of 'soft rationalism' : a rational formal framework and an internal rationality which easily accommodates contingent or accidental elements and can absorb constructional connotations and linguistic variations.[38]

The cooperative attitude that Fortis brings forth is exemplified by his relationship with a group of former students. Since 1979, he has shared his office with Adalberto Caccia, Paolo Colombo, Rita Mangone, and Paolo Monti, and on occasion they have collaborated in the preparation of specific projects.

The educational careers and professional development of Giancarlo Motta and Antonia Pizzigoni have been closely tied to the leading exponents of the *Tendenza*. Both Motta and Pizzigoni, 1970 graduates of the Polytechnic in Milan, have collaborated in some manner with Aldo Rossi, Danièle Vitale, and Massimo Fortis (Pizzigoni collaborated with Rossi in the design of the row houses in Mozzo, outside of Bergamo). In their professional activities, Motta-Pizzigoni have to this day focused primarily on academic and theoretical investigations. As disciples of Rossi, they have investigated the morphology of urban areas, in particular the developments immediately on the periphery of the historic centers of the city:

In the study of the contemporary city, we have focused on the areas of the first expansions, and in the recent expansions of Milan. We have altered, therefore, the priority usually given in urban studies to the historic centers....[39]

At the Milan Polytechnic, Motta leads one of the research teams with Fortis and Vitale. Their focus has been on the urban block as the primary organizing element in the city. In their investigations of the Garibaldi-Isola area in the southwest part of Milan, they have isolated a limited number of building types which are then abstracted and reintroduced to the area. Similar results are obtained in investigations of other Milanese neighborhoods, such as Porta Genova and Porta Ticinese. The work by Motta and Pizzigoni outside of teaching has been urban competitions which to date have not resulted in commissions. Three that stand out are the proposal for the urban park of Porto Navile in Bologna of 1985, the community plaza project in Nembri (BE), also of 1985, and the 1986 proposal for a new plaza and restoration of the Castello in Orzinuovi in Brescia province. Their work is rigorously developed, based on very specific typologies. The plaza in Orzinuovi, for example, is based on a gate, a tower, and a loggia. The composition of these elements on the castle grounds, to the exterior of the historic city core, extend the Roman axis from the center to the eastern suburbs.

Luca Scacchetti's work is very significant since it illustrates an intellectual and professional dedication to the formal qualities of autochthonous architecture. Younger than the others, he has had a very active career which has involved design at various levels, from furniture to urban building façades. Each design has a history, or at least is based on an understanding of that particular typology. His training was Milan, finishing in 1975 with a thesis project for collective housing in the Garibaldi-Isola area. Scacchetti now teaches at the Polytechnic and continues the type of typological investigations he carried out as a student. Principal among these is his study of building typologies and urban morphologies in the Valsassina area of Lake Como. This very exhaustive investigation has catalogued multiple variations of a large number of types, from small country-side oratory chapels to rural house forms and town structures.

Collectively, the architects whose work is included represent a very small part of the total number of practitioners in Ticino, Piedmont, and Lombardy. Just in the canton of Ticino there are two hundred practicing architects, so the handful that are included here are a small minority. What is astounding is the quality of the work of these few. They represent the best of a generation of architects who do not blindly reject the tenets of the modern movement without regard to their validity or applicability. The work of these architects, from the generation that began its professional activities in the 1950s to those only now beginning, illustrates the possibilities of an architecture based in tradition *and* in innovation, an architecture that neither imitates nor mimics. It is an architecture that gives order to the public realm and identity to private space.

Linescio (TI): detail of the entry into an old rustici

NOTES

1. The designations for the political subdivisions of Switzerland and Italy are:
TI—canton Ticino, Switzerland
BE—Bergamo province (Lombardy region), Italy
BO—Bologna province (Emilia Romagna region), Italy
BR—Brescia province (Lombardy region), Italy
CO—Como province (Lombardy region), Italy
CR—Crema province (Lombardy region), Italy
MA—Mantova province (Lombardy region), Italy
MI—Milan province (Lombardy region), Italy
MO—Modena province (Emilia Romagna region), Italy
NO—Novara province (Piedmont region), Italy
PA—Pavia province (Lombardy region), Italy
RE—Reggio Emilia province (Emilia Romagna region), Italy
VA—Varese province (Lombardy region), Italy.

2. Kenneth Frampton, Modern Architecture: A Critical History, revised and enlarged edition (London: Thames and Hudson, 1985), 294.

3. Emil Kaufmann, *Von Ledoux bis Le Corbusier: Ursprung und Entwicklung der Autonomen Architektur* (quoted from the Spanish edition, *De Ledoux a Le Corbusier: Origen y desarrollo de la arquitectura autónoma*. Barcelona: Editorial Gustavo Gili, 1982, 72–76).

4. *The American Heritage Dictionary of the English Language* (Boston, MA: Houghton Mifflin Co., 1976), 1343. The name in German and French is Tessin; for cultural reasons, its Italian name is used in this *Guide*.

5. The reference is to the architecture of the 1920s and 1930s by Le Corbusier, Walter Gropius, Ludwig Mies van der Rohe, J.J.P. Oud, and others. A useful source of information on this period is Reyner Banham, *Theory and Design in the First Machine Age* (New York: Praeger Publishers, 1960).

6. Kenneth Frampton, "Mario Botta and the School of the Ticino," *Oppositions 14* (1978): 2. See also his introduction, "The

Will to Build," in *Mario Botta: Architecture and Projects in the '70* (Milano: Electa Editrice, 1979), 7.

7. *Sopra Ceneri* refers to the region north of Monte Ceneri, the mountain that separates the northern valleys of the Ticino River and the Piano di Maggadino (Maggadino plain) from the area to the south or *sotto Ceneri*. Italian geographers simply identify the alpine and pre-alpine regions.

8. Interview with Snozzi (15 October 1986). This perception was echoed by various other architects who were interviewed.

9. Included in the bibliography are a number of works that are particularly helpful in developing an overall impression of the characteristics of these constructions.

10. Werner Blaser, *Architecture 70/80 in Switzerland* (Basel/Boston/Stuttgart: Birkhäuser Verlag, 1981), 17.

11. *Rustici* are rural structures, literally farmhouses. In Switzerland, this includes any rural, rustic structure found in the small villages, hamlets, and older towns, where they also served as storage sheds and so on. In Italy, and particularly in relation to the structures in the Lombardian and Piedmontese plains, the term applies to farm annexes in which the farmhands live and in which are also stored the farm equipment (Giorgio Grassi, " 'Rural' y 'urbano' en la arquitectura," *La arquitectura como oficio y otros escritos*. Barcelona: Editorial Gustavo Gili, S.A., 1977, 157).

12. In the first paragraph of his introduction to the catalogue *Illuminismo e architettura del '700 veneto*, Aldo Rossi states that the purpose for the essay is to "put forth an interest, and a tendency of the past and the present, for an architecture of reason" ("La arquitectura de la razón como arquitectura de tendencia," *Para una arquitectura de tendencia: escritos 1956-1972*. Barcelona: Editorial Gustavo Gili, 1977, 231). This is but one of various writings where the design approach is identified as "of tendency."

13. Aldo Rossi, *L'architettura della città* (Padova: Marsilio Editori, 1966). Translated to Spanish (*La arquitectura de la ciudad*. Barcelona: Editorial Gustavo Gili, 1971), German (*Die Architektur des Stadt, Skizze zu einer grundlegenden Theorie des Urbanen*. Düsseldorf: Verlagsgruppe Bertelsmann GmbH, 1973), Portuguese (*A Ar-*

quitectura da cidade. Lisboa: Edições Cosmos, 1977), and English (*The Architecture of the City*. Cambridge, MA: The MIT Press, 1982). Other writings by Rossi include a collection of essays, *Scritti scelti sull' architettura e la città*: 1956-1972 (Milano: CLUP, 1975), a Spanish translation, *Para una arquitectura de tendencia* (Barcelona, 1977), and *A Scientific Autobiography* (Cambridge, MA: The MIT Press, 1981).

Giorgio Grassi, *La costruzione logica dell' architettura* (Padova: 1967; Spanish edition, *La construcción lógica de la arquitectura*. Barcelona: Colegio Oficial de Arquitectos de Cataluña y Baleares, 1973). A collection of essays was mentioned above, published in Spanish as *La arquitectura como oficio y otros escritos*.

Vittorio Gregotti: *Il territorio dell' architettura* (Milano: 1966).

14. *La arquitectural como oficio*, 143–57. "The licence of obviousness," *Lotus International*, no. 15 (June 1977): 26–27 (Spanish translation, "Nota sobre la arquitectura rural," *La arquitectural como oficio*, 193–95).

15. Originally published in 1979 by the Fondazione Ticino Nostro in a limited edition and long out of print, this study has been recently re-published in abbreviated form as *La costruzione del territorio: Uno studio sul Canton Ticino* (Milano: CLUP, 1985).

16. Luca Scacchetti, letter of 20 February 1987.

17. Giancarlo Motta and Antonia Pizzigoni, "La questión de la manzana en la construcción de la periferia de Milán," *La manzana como idea de ciudad* (Barcelona: 2C Ediciones): 64–73, and *La casa e la città* (Milano: CLUP, 1987).

18. The final year project of Bonicalzi and Braghieri focused on residential typology. Grassi, "Tipología residencial en Pavia," in *La arquitectura como oficio*, 93–95.

19. Interview with L. Snozzi (Locarno, 15 October 1986).

20. Aurelio Galfetti, "Conservare = transformare," *Rivista Tecnica*, no. 12 (December 1986): 27.

21. Tita Carloni, quoted in Kenneth Frampton, *Modern Architecture: A Critical History*, rev. ed. (New York: Thames and Hudson, 1985), 322.

22. Tita Carloni, "Architecture of the Wall and not of the Trilith: Building in Mario Botta," *Lotus International*, No. 37 (I, 1983): 35.

23. Interview with A. Galfetti (Bellinzona, 13 October 1986).

24. "Notes of a Design Process," in *Luigi Snozzi: Urban Renewal at Monte Carasso* (London: 9H Gallery, 1986), 5.

25. Werner Seligmann discusses this briefly in his critique published with a portfolio of work, "The mountains and the machine," *Progressive Architecture* 63, no. 7 (July 1982): 64–71.

26. Mario Campi, "The Commitment to Tradition," *Mario Campi - Franco Pessina, Architects* (New York: Rizzoli International, 1987), 16.

27. *Ibid.*

28. Manfredo Tafuri, "Adventures of the Object: The Architecture of Vittorio Gregotti," in *Vittorio Gregotti, Buildings and Projects* (New York: Rizzoli International, 1982), 21.

29. *Vittorio Gregotti, Buildings and Projects*, 93–96.

30. Quoted in Frampton, *Modern Architecture: A Critical History*, 295.

31. "Canaletto and Aldo Rossi: The Relationship Between Painting and Architectural Creation," *Modulus/The University of Virginia School of Architecture Review* (1982), 83.

32. Aldo Rossi, "An Analogical Architecture," *A+U* (Architecture and Urbanism) no. 65 (May, 1976):74.

33. Interview in *L' Architettura* 360, vol. XXXI, no. 10 (October 1985): 748.

34. *L' Architettura* 360.

35. "Rudy Hunziker, or Architecture as a Manifestation of Continuity (introduction to exhibition catalogue)," in *Rudy Hunziker* (Old Westbury, NY: New York Institute of Technology, 1986), 11.

36. Hunziker is Adjunct Professor of Architecture at the Virginia Polytechnic Institute and State University in Blacksburg, Virginia.

37. Quoted in "Rehabilitation of Boarding School, Novara, 1975," 9H, no. 5 (1983): 74.

38. "Rehabilitation of Boarding School."

39. Giancarlo Motta and Antonia Pizzigoni, "La questión de la manzana en la construcción de la periferia de Milán," 66.

Museo Civico: *View of the castle*

Bellinzona and Carasso

1.1 Museo Civico, Castello di Montebello 1974
Salita ai Castelli, 4, Bellinzona
tel. (092) 25-13-42
Mario Campi, Franco Pessina, and Niki Piazzoli
Open Tuesday to Sunday, 10–12, 14–17; admission charged.

1.2 Castelgrande (restoration) since 1984
Piazza del Sole (elevator access), Bellinzona
tel. (092) 25-42-96
Aurelio Galfetti
The castle is undergoing renovation; the elevator access is available from the Piazza del Sole, and the castle can also be reached by foot from the historic center by following a clearly marked pedestrian path.

1.3 Bagno pubblico comunale 1967–70
Via Mirasole, Bellinzona
tel. (092) 25-73-34
Aurelio Galfetti, Flora Ruchat, and Ivo Trümpy
The community swimming complex is open during the summer months; the bridge is accessible year-round.

1.4 Centro tennistico comunale 1984–86
Via Brunari, Bellinzona
tel. (092) 26-20-20
Aurelio Galfetti
Open throughout the week during the season, 8:00–18:00.

1.5 Centro postale 1977–85
Viale Stazione, 15, Bellinzona
tel. (092) 24-61-11
Aurelio Galfetti, Angelo Bianchi, and Renato Molina
The public areas are open during business hours, Monday to Saturday.

1.6 Villa on Via Mirasole 1985
Via Mirasole, 4, Bellinzona
Aurelio Galfetti
Private; visible from the street.

1.7 Casa Bianca/Casa Nera 1986–87
Via Vicenzo d'Alberti, Bellinzona
Aurelio Galfetti
Private; visible from the street and the public spaces around the two houses.

1.8 Casa Minotti 1982–83
Vicolo Parè, Carasso
Ivano Gianola
Private; access from the center of town; the house is visible from the street. Can be seen from across the valley, especially from the Castello di Montebello.

The city of Bellinzona exists because of the mountains, at a point where the valley widens and the Ticino River turns west along the Piano di Magadino to form Lago Maggiore. Bellinzona, with its complex of three castles and the connecting fortified walls, was the barrier that controlled access to the three high mountain passes of San Gottardo, San Bernardino, and Lucomagno. Castelgrande, the oldest of the three castles, is a small-scale acropolis fifty meters above the valley floor; it has been fortified since the late fourth century and is currently under restoration. Castello di Montebello, ninety meters above the Castelgrande, was begun in the late thirteenth century. Castello di Sasso Corbaro, 230 meters above the city, is a typical Sforza fortification built by the Dukes of Milan in 1479. Fragments of the city enclosure abound, from the Castello di Sasso Corbaro to the western slopes across the river in Carasso; the morphology of the city and its immediate suburbs is still very much affected by this history.

The castles remain an important part of the city's living structure. In 1974 the donjon and the manor house of the Castello di Montebello were converted into an archaeological museum. In their formal response, Mario Campi, Franco Pessina, and Niki Piazzoli inserted the new elements in contraposition to the existing structure. The dialogue that this established is carried throughout in a very clear manner: the old stone walls are thick, heavy, and barely perforated; the new insert is a lightweight steel structure, its floor slabs and glass display cases suspended from the top of the old. The dialogue between old and new is reinforced by the gap that separates the new insert from the castle's walls.

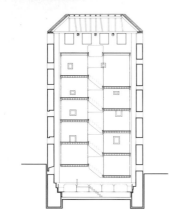

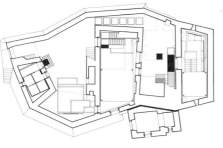

Museo Civico
Interior view
*Section through the
donjon or keep*
*View of the court between
the donjon and the mansion*
Entry floor plan

After its restoration by Aurelio Galfetti, the Castelgrande will house banquet rooms, a restaurant, exhibition halls, and meeting rooms within its wings, while its grounds will provide a city park. Begun in 1984, the work includes new emergency stairs and elevator access from the Piazza del Sole to the castle yard. The circulation spine through the solid granite rock begins the dialogue envisioned by Galfetti between old and new, between city and fortress, between man-made objects and nature. At the top, the two elevators open to a small plaza adjacent to the fortification wall. The project is "first of all a search for a new significance for the fortress in its relationship with the town and with history."[1] What Galfetti is preserving is the presence of the walls and towers on the skyline of the city; the new functions and interventions clearly are such, and make no attempt to mimic elements that have long disappeared.

Aurelio Galfetti, in association with Flora Ruchat and Ivo Trümpy, designed the community swimming complex in 1967–70. It now forms the central spine of a recreational complex that includes Galfetti's new tennis club (1984–86) as well as the existing soccer football stadium and ice skating rink. The central organizational element of the swimming complex is a double wall, a bridge or viaduct which alludes to the fortified enclosure of Bellinzona as it provides access from the parking areas to the various swimming pools. The organization of the complex also inverts Le Corbusier's notion of pedestrian and vehicular separation: in this case it is the vehicles that remain on the ground and the bridge that carries pedestrians across from one to another point. The layout permits access to the three distinct swimming areas, one being for recreational swimming, one providing a shallow pool for toddlers, and a third

Castelgrande (restoration)
View of the upper elevator entry
View from Castello Montebello

offering a competition area with separate ten meter diving basin and Olympic pool. Changing rooms and other support facilities are located below the spine, accessible down two stairs which serve as control points. The reinforced concrete spine is six meters above the meadow, and the changing rooms, built of steel with wood floor deck and prefabricated in-

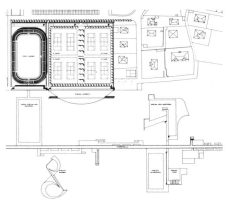

Bagno pubblico comunale
View from the lawn
Aerial view
*General site plan including the tennis
center, proposed indoor swimming pool,
and proposed ice skating rink*

fill panels, form the intermediate level to the ground. This allows for unimpeded movement between the areas of the complex at ground level.

Galfetti's community tennis center also explores the idea of parallel walls derived from the morphology of Bellinzona. Here the relationship is perpendicular rather than axial, analogous to entry into the city as one approaches from the parking lot to the tennis courts. The outside world of the city is separated from the inside world of recreation by the double wall onto which are attached the various ancillary facilities of this center. The top of the parallel walls corresponds to the sentry's walk along the fortification walls: here this walk provides access to the changing rooms of the tennis center. Its structure is exposed reinforced concrete. Any surface texture and decoration on the walls result from Galfetti's concern with the dimensional characteristics of the form work used in casting and from the expansion of concrete through the joints of the form work without blocking. Galfetti uses this characteristic to form a horizontal extrusion from the wall plane, creating a pattern of alternating light and shadow.

The new postal building which houses the regional distribution center and offices is deliberately subdued, treated as a typical infill structure. Aurelio Galfetti rejects the new structure as a monument. Its façade is

Centro tennistico comunale
View of the entry from the parking lot
View of the building from the tennis courts

anonymous, an element simply to continue the existing street wall. In section, the new post office is a typical building against the wall of the mountain. Where one gains space between building and mountain, the solution is to create semi-private courts; in other cases, the structure is only centimeters away from the rock. Its plan forms an H. Two courts at either end function according to the particular condition: the court to the north, exposed by the diagonal Via Daro, faces a public parking lot and constitutes the forecourt to a snack bar. The open space to the south is reached from Viale Stazione through a private drive. Along Viale Stazione the façade is subtilely articulated by minute changes in the plane of the wall, the changing band colors, and is accentuated by a deep cornice. Seen from the Castello di Montebello, the post office presents a different story. First, the building reads as a hollowed quadrilateral with a continuous gable roof cut off to expose courtyards at both ends. Second, there is a gabled volume within the central space of the quadrilateral which is separated from the perimeter by two void elements; these are dissected by three perpendicular gables. The building, then, reads both as a nondescript street wall and as a carved solid revealing its components. A central entrance from Viale Stazione leads past the perimeter zone housing the secondary public functions such as telegraph office and mailboxes, and proceeds into the high volume interstitial space containing the service windows.

Three recent multi-family structures by Aurelio Galfetti indicate a departure

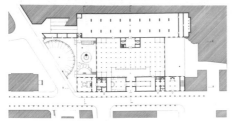

Centro postale
View of the north end
Ground floor plan
Interior view of the public lobby

Villa on Via Mirasole
View from Via Mirasole

from the typical and anonymous multi-family housing slabs of the 1960s and 1970s. The three houses are located on residential streets to the south of the historic center, and are a thematic exploration by Galfetti that transforms free-standing, symmetrical cubes. Theirs is an architecture of layers, where the outer skin is peeled and carved to expose differentiated wall finishes. All three are constructed in reinforced concrete and use granite to give articulation to the exterior layer. The first villa is on Via Mirasole. After the forms were removed from the dark outside walls, horizontal granite stripes were added, concealing the construction joints. These control the scale of the façade, and increase the contrast with the exposed interior planes, which are finished in white. The house is a biaxially symmetrical cube, entered on axis from Via Mirasole. Vertical circulation is located at the center. Each of the principal façades, toward Via Mirasole or the garden, has a remnant columnar fin on center, framed by the two solid end towers, while the rest of the volume has been carved away. The side elevations are nearly solid, with pairs of vertical slits along the center axis on

Casa Bianca

Casa Nera

the lower three floors and near the edge on the upper story. There are eight nearly identical duplex dwellings within the volume. The bottom four have ground level terraces and gardens, the upper four units have roof terraces. All consist of an L plan; the services are located within the central zone.

Galfetti's two most recent villas on Via Vicenzo d'Alberti continue the thematic and technical explorations of the villa on Via Mirasole. In their construction, the Casa Bianca and Casa Nera are similar to the first, although in this case, Galfetti deals with the control of joints on the form work by inserting the granite strips prior to pouring the concrete, so that they act as blocking between sections of forms and become part of the wall. One house has a lighter add-mixture than the other, so that the appearance of one is of a black cube with light gray bands, and the other, a light gray with black bands. In the two examples, these elements are not additive, but integrative. The two structures are a refinement of the villa on Via Mirasole in the manner in which the volume is carved, in the disposition and type of dwellings.

A restoration by Ivano Gianola in Carasso presents an iconographic solution to the problem of adapting a nondescript structure on a dramatic site.

On the western slopes across the Ticino river from Bellinzona, the cantonal capital, the location of this small house makes it very desirable. The original house is a two-room deep, two story structure with a central hall and stairway; Gianola retains this plan in his renovation, though he converts what had been an attic space into part of a double volume central hall. The exterior changes make this house noteworthy. Gianola clarifies the archetypal relationship between base, body and top by encircling the lower front of the house with horizontal bands of alternating colors, simplifying its top with a hip roof, and introducing brow windows just below the overhang. He further formalizes the façade facing Bellinzona by constructing double stairs which lead to the central door.

Casa Minotti:
Front elevation

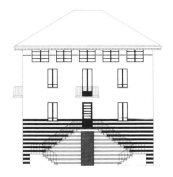

Valle Leventina

2.1 San Gottardo-Sud service area 1985–87
N2 highway, northbound, outside Airolo
Tita Carloni with Aurelio Galfetti and others
Public; open at all times.

2.2 Single family house 1984–85
Ambri town center, immediately behind the parish church
Pietro Boschetti
Private.

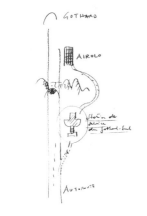

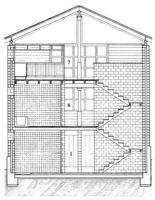

***San Gottardo-Sud
service area***
*Exterior view looking north
Sketch plan by Tita Carloni*

**Single-family house,
Ambri**
Section

The superhighway N2, which dissects the canton of Ticino, connects the rest of Switzerland with northern Italy. Where the northbound half of the road enters the long tunnel of San Gottardo near Airolo, a new service area was completed in 1987. Designed by Tita Carloni with Aurelio Galfetti and others, this modest complex reflects the Ticinese architects' concern for clarity of structure, form, and function. The axially symmetrical composition of the plan places the gasoline pumps under a large roof in front of the T-shaped building. The main entrance is a projecting central element which leads to the shopping area and restaurant. Typical of the architects' work, the construction materials of this service area are immaculately detailed.

Located in the center of the village of Ambri, high along the Leventina valley north of Bellinzona, a small, single-family house designed by Pietro Boschetti and built in 1984 transforms the traditional village building form while retaining its fundamental characteristics. It is a cubic, gabled structure with the gable ends facing the streets, its dimensions based on those of the typical *rustici*. The layout of the house is straightforward: the entrance and service spaces—studio, laundry, storage, and pantry—are located in the lower level, the sleeping rooms are located in the middle level, while the group spaces—living, dining, and kitchen—are assigned to the spacious volume of the upper floor that extends into what would otherwise be an attic space.

Monte Carasso

3.1 Palestra 1981–84
North of the town square, Monte Carasso
tel. (092) 25-37-84
Luigi Snozzi
Inquire at the town hall for hours when the gymnasium can be visited.

3.2 Cassa Raiffeisen 1980–84
Town square, Monte Carasso
tel. (092) 26-33-23
Luigi Snozzi
The bank lobby can be visited during office hours; on the door to the house above a sign reads: "Non si ricevono turisti d'architettura"— tourists of architecture are not welcomed!

3.3 Casa Guidotti 1983–84
East of the town square, Monte Carasso
tel. (092) 25-37-84
Luigi Snozzi
Private, but the house is free-standing and visible from public spaces.

Monte Carasso
View of the center of town from the cemetery
Master plan by Luigi Snozzi, showing his interventions

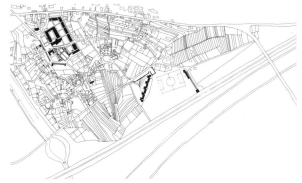

The cadastral map of Monte Carasso indicates a village composed of highly irregular parcels. The element which gives the village any urban order is the old church and cloister; the layout of the cemetery is askew to this. Monte Carasso is typical of towns and villages near larger cities which undergo unimaginative sprawl as they are transformed into bedroom communities. Luigi Snozzi has been involved in the preparation and implementation of the master plan for the village since 1977. Though his first proposed project was Casa Verdemonte, an apartment building designed in 1974 (the present building was executed by others), Snozzi's involvement began in earnest with the competition project for a school which, according to a 1965 development plan, was to be placed in the periphery of the town. Instead, Snozzi proposed to place the new school within the town, as part of the existing medieval monastery. The ensuing discussion led to a referendum which disapproved the official development plan. Snozzi was appointed to develop a master plan, and the result is one which gives order to the medieval town in a clearly non-historicist manner. This involves the insertion of specific structures that, with the church and cloister-cum-school,

will create a new order and reinforce the notion of a formal center with public space defined by public functions.

Snozzi completes the atrium of the monastery with a new wing forming part of the school. He further proposes new parceling of land as existing structures become vacant and new ones are built to the north of the church; this will give a clear definition to the heart of the village by enclosing the church complex with green open space. The sports hall (1981–84) begins this new apportionment. Other structures in the master plan are the new bank building (1980–84), the Guidotti House (1983–84), the columbarium of the cemetery (1983), the new stands and changing rooms for the soccer field on the northern edge of the town (1983–86), the proposed kindergarten that will form the eastern limit of the central square, and extensions to the cemetery for reconciliation of its geometry to the new orthogonal grid of the village center. He also has renovated the existing town hall to the west of the town center. Snozzi states that "the aim of the plan is the phased comprehensive requalification of the central core of the town, as a public place par excellence."[2]

The new gymnasium is the first realized in Snozzi's restructuring plan for the center of Monte Carasso. The required areas of the building are divided into two volumes, and Snozzi uses the

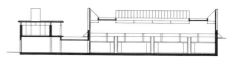

Palestra
View of the gymnasium complex from the south
Interior of the gymnasium
Section through the entry house and gymnasium

change of grade to diminish the scale of the gymnasium itself by placing the floor level below grade. From the town center, the gymnasium is an element which projects above an outdoor terrace (a basketball court); the entry building houses the changing rooms, as well as the shelter and other community facilities, and serves as a portico, its exterior staircase the connector to the northeast part of town. Because of

Cassa Raiffeisen: *front elevation*

Casa Guidotti: *view from the cemetery*

its immaculate design and precision of construction, Snozzi's new gymnasium in Monte Carasso was awarded in 1985 a prize for construction in concrete.[3]

The Cassa Raiffeisen building includes a private residence above the savings bank. The division of the three floors of the building creates a split-level house that is rather like a Corbusian Unité in section, and a banking level which has a high volume public lobby balancing the more intimate private area. In the basement are located the bank's meeting room and the required shelters. Its rectangular main façade has a square cut out. Glass surrounds a square insert with protruding curved eaves; at its center is the entry to the bank, a vault-like door. In the master plan, the bank building is part of a continuous building wall defining the south edge of the central square.

The house for the mayor of Monte Carasso, Flavio Guidotti, is a tower structure which articulates the eastern boundary of the town center. Its garden wall will form the edge of a proposed new perimeter street to complete this boundary. Snozzi alludes to the domino frame of Le Corbusier's single-family house at the Weissenhofsiedlung in his design, although clearly he is not replicating this masterpiece. In its orientation, the Guidotti House responds at

right angles to the principal axis of the site: the main façade opens northeast to the garden. In plan, the living spaces are placed on this side of the house; the other façade, to the public side, remains rather closed, and it is in here where the services are located. The entry and a combination living, eating, and cooking space are at ground level; on the first floor above, the master bedroom and an office that overlooks the downstairs; three other bedrooms are located on the second floor, and a roof terrace exists at the top.

The structures by Luigi Snozzi in Monte Carasso are a clear continuation of the vocabulary of the masters of the modern movement. However, there is more to the designs of these new buildings. In Snozzi's architecture, the clarity of the granite stone of the traditional structures is transliterated to reinforced concrete construction, a reflection of the traditions and conditions that preexist in Monte Carasso and elsewhere. In addition, the notion of typology is basic for Snozzi when dealing with public spaces and structures for everyday life, since the variety of uses of these public places do not change. The definition of the town center, therefore, is an attempt to give clarity to the primary space, to create a public square surrounded by public functions.

41

Camorino

Casa Del Curto: *View
from the garden*

Camorino is typical of those villages and towns adjacent to main highways. The town has grown as
people have sought housing away from Bellinzona
because of its convenient access to the nearby superhighway. The Del Curto House by Antonio Bassi,
Giovanni Gherra, and Dario Galimberti (1984–85)
is among residences recently built in the new subdivisions. As is typical in their recent work, the
house is based on abstract historical allusions—their
references are to French Rationalism of the
nineteenth century—rather than the Ticinese *rustici*.
In this house for the family Del Curto, the reference
is to Ledoux's architecture, such as his proposed
villa for a merchant from Besançon. Bassi-Gherra-
Galimberti's solution presents a sedate answer to the
problem of placing a house which retains a sense of
identity and quiet presence in the midst of suburban
sprawl. It is a Palladian villa in plan, with a very
traditional distribution of spaces: ground level entry,
vertical circulation and a double-volumed hall on
center, with the kitchen, study, eating, and living
spaces to either side. On the upper floor, sleeping
and bath rooms flank the central volume, with a U-
shaped hall bridging to the balcony overlooking the
garden. This main façade faces south, and its central
portion is articulated by a Serliana above a rectangular recess and below a central oculus. This formal
motif is reinforced by the color scheme of the
façade. The area of the wall immediately above the
Serliana is painted a light yellow. This contrasts
with the light blue color used on the majority of
the exterior surfaces. A subtle articulation on the
façade surface creates abstracted giant order,
corner pilasters which are painted white. All
metal elements—window frames, railings, and
downspouts—are painted red. Other than this, the

detailing of the house is very spartan, including the interior.

There are two other projects worth noting, both located to the west of the town center: an elementary school by Fonso and Pietro Boschetti and Fosco Moretti (1977–78) and a single family house by Ivo Trümpy (1979). The elementary school is organized with its central space and hallways forming an H in plan. Classrooms and other spaces are placed to the outside and between the legs, while the commons in the center is covered by a pyramidal skylight. In contrast to the school and the house by Bassi-Gherra-Galimberti, the Lüönd House by Ivo Trümpy is best described as an attempt at designing in a somewhat vernacular manner while inverting the roof arrangement so that the house looks more like a transformed Ferraran rural house. The house is designed as an energy efficient structure, with the services on the north side and all the living spaces facing south. Construction is of modular concrete block with wood supports for the balcony and roof structure.

Casa Del Curto
Above left: Combination axonometric view
Middle: Interior of the central space

Scuole elementari comunali
Above right: General view from the west
Below left: Interior showing the central space

North of the Ticino River: Cugnasco and Gerra-Piano

5.1 Casa Calzascia 1982–83
Via Sciarana, Cugnasco
Franco and Paolo Moro
Private; visible from the street.

5.2 Casa Viggiano 1970–72
Via Sciarana, Cugnasco
Ivano Gianola
Private; the south façade is visible from the road below.

5.3 Casa Heschl 1983–84
Agarone, above Gerra-Piano
Luigi Snozzi
Private; visible from below and from public paths, since access to the house is by a public trail.

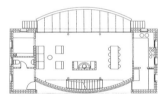

Casa Calzascia
View facing the Piano di Magadino
Main floor plan
Upside-down axonometric

The towns of Cugnasco and Gerra Piano are on the north border of the Piano di Magadino along the highway between Monte Carasso and Locarno, separated from one another by the creek that flows down the Valle di Cugnasco. The Calzascia House by Franco and Paolo Moro (1982–83) in Cugnasco is situated on one of the roads leading up the hill. The structure is sited parallel to the slope, with all its principal spaces facing south towards the view. The house is organized with two solid ends containing the kitchen, bathrooms, and storage spaces. Volumetrically, it is a traditional house which has been carved away; in plan the north wall of the principal volume is a segmental arc tangential to the overall rectangle. This is replicated on the opposite side by the veranda. The construction is concrete block with wood joists and metal roofing. The southern façade is nearly all glass between the solid ends, while the rest of the structure is basically solid with limited perforations. In its detailing and selection of materials, this is an immaculate and crisp structure.

A project by Ivano Gianola, the Viggiano House (1970–71), can be found further up the same road. It is a reinforced concrete structure with heavy overhangs, now covered with vines, clearly influenced by Le Corbusier's Brutalist architecture. Its plan is rectangular, with the spaces distributed over four floors. The middle two levels of the house contain the family spaces and open through a double volume of the living room past the brise-soleil to the view. The master bedroom suite and studio are above, as is the entrance into the house.

The Heschl House by Luigi Snozzi (1983–84) is located in the Agarone area up the mountain from Gerra-Piano, on a site adjacent to the creek and overlooking the Piano di Magadino. It is reached from a public path that begins at the fifth switch-back of the road. Entry to the house is through a portal and across a bridge structure which is oriented at forty-five degrees to the body of the building. The exposed concrete house appears to be a buried cube that encloses a small archetypal tower. The principal space is a high volume that extends into the pyramidal roof above, with the secondary spaces arranged around it.

Casa Heschl
View from the approach
View from the back of the house toward the Piano di Magadino

Cadenazzo, San Antonino and San Nazzaro

6.1 Casa Caccia 1970–71
East of the municipal parking lot, Cadenazzo
Mario Botta
Private; house is visible from the road.

6.2 Single-family house 1980
East of the municipal parking lot, Cadenazzo
Antonio Bassi, Giovanni Gherra, and Dario Galimberti
Private; house is visible from the road.

6.3 Single-family house 1984–85
Across from the train station, San Antonino
Franco and Paolo Moro
Private; house is visible from the road.

6.4 Scuola elementare e municipio 1973–78
Town center, San Nazzaro
tel. (093) 63-14-08
Luigi Snozzi
The municipal offices are open Monday to Friday, 9–11, as well as Tuesday afternoons, 14–18; visitors should ask for permission to visit the academic section of the building in the school office. Grounds are open and accessible year-round. Public spaces surround the building.

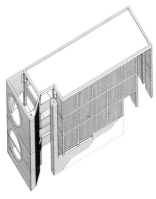

Casa Caccia
View from above toward the Piano di Magadino
Axonometric view

The growth that Cadenazzo and San Antonino have experienced, as with other villages along major highways, is mostly in the form of uninspiring subdivisions of formerly agricultural land. Both towns are particularly desirable locations as they are adjacent to the federal highway between Bellinzona and Lugano as well as the road that leads to the towns on the southeastern shore of Lago Lugano. San Antonino is also near the entrance to the superhighway to Lugano. San Nazzaro, to the west, is a village on the southeastern shore of the lake that has relatively easy access to both Locarno and Lugano. Facing north, it views the hillside developments across the lake.

Within a new subdivision to the north of the village center of Cadenazzo are two houses, the Caccia House by Mario Botta (1970–71) and the single-family house by Antonio Bassi, Giovanni Gherra, and Dario Galimberti (1980). Both are well designed projects. The Caccia House is sited perpendicular to the site. Two floors accommodate the living spaces; on the top floors the private rooms are separated from one another by a void open to the space below. All the service spaces, including stairs and bathrooms, are placed against the glass block wall of the west façade. The house by Bassi-Gherra-Galimberti is symmetrical about its pedimented frontispiece, a response that is typical of their work. The disposition of spaces is more traditional, though here too there is some visual connection between the two floors of the house. While Botta's design clearly tries to block the view of the adjacent structures, a camera obscura that focuses only on the mountains beyond, the structure by Bassi et al. responds in a very traditional and iconographic manner to the requirements; both show

Casa Caccia:
View from below

Single-family house, Cadenazzo
View from the garden

an attitude that one can say is appropriate under the circumstances.

On the Piano itself, a single-family house by the Moro brothers (1984–85) is located in a recently subdivided area of San Antonino. The train station is located across the road to the north, and, until recently, an industrial complex was found to the west. Mountains are to the north and south of the valley floor, but the adjacent houses block the view. The Moro brothers have therefore organized this house so that its views are restricted with the primary orientation to the west. In plan the house is a segment of a circle with a rectangular element attached to the cord. The arced back wall is a solid plain against which the stairs and the general circulation space are located. The various house functions are distributed in a traditional manner, with the family living spaces on the lower level and the individual rooms above.

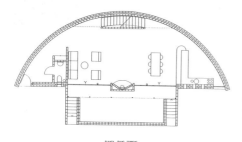

Single-family house, San Antonino
View of the west front
Interior view
Main floor plan

Top right: **Single-family house, Cadenazzo**
View from the street

A basement houses the mechanical room and storage areas. The rectangular element is a loggia and terrace that serves the sleeping and group areas. Its scale and size are deceiving. What is most visible is the nearly solid block arc, punctuated every tenth course and five block lengths by square glass block. From the west, the ends of the curved wall form solid pillars framing a vertical band of glass. These are separated from the two-square loggia-terrace by solid walls.

Among Luigi Snozzi's urban interventions is a new civic center for San Nazzaro, a town on the south shore of Lago Maggiore. The new school and municipal office building (1973–78) continues an architectural theme found in other of his structures. As with these other buildings, this structure is reinforced concrete. The complex has a square plan, formed by the equilateral L of the building proper defining the public formal square. The square terminates a grand pedestrian spine leading from the community church. This path takes one past the cemetery, along private homes that will be removed to create a green space, and past the old, neoclassical building formerly occupied by the municipal offices and school.

The location of this axis is established by an existing retaining wall found behind the old municipal building. Each side of the new structure houses a different function. The

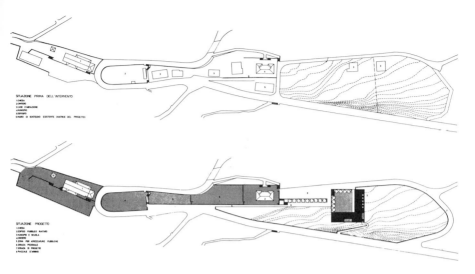

**Scuola elementare e municipio,
San Nazzaro**
*Top: Site plans, before and proposed
Left: Interior view of the
municipal offices
Right: View of the southeast corner*

municipal offices are housed in the
wing that is the terminus of the
pedestrian spine; perpendicular to this
is the new primary school. The
municipal wing is organized off of a
single loaded, double volume corridor.
Its administrative offices are located on
the main level, while a community
meeting room is found above, overlooking the hallway. On the other hand, the
barbell, split level plan of the school
separates the central entry hall from
the classroom spaces.

Locarno

7.1 Scuole e palestra comunali Saleggi 1971–74 (school), **1979**
(gymnasium)
Via Nessi and Via E. Pestalozzi, Locarno
tel. (093) 31-65-82
Livio Vacchini
Open during the academic year; visitors should ask for permission to visit the buildings in the school office. Grounds are open and accessible year-round.

7.2 Atelier Vacchini 1985
Via Bramantino 33, Locarno
tel. (092) 25-13-42
Livio Vacchini
The architect's office.

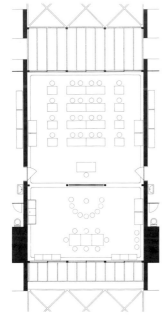

Scuole e palestra comunali Saleggi
View of the gymnasium
Detail floor plan of typical classroom module

Located on the northern end of Lago Maggiore, this resort city still retains its historic core. However, its contemporary constructions have not provided the city with a clear and cohesive direction. Near the lake front and around the transportation terminals ground-level arcades are cluttered with tourist shops, while mediocre new buildings crowd into the historic fabric of Locarno, their sole purpose being to provide efficient commercial space. Above the city, the hillsides are a serpentine mass of apartments and single family structures along narrow roads, all competing for the southern exposure and lake view.

There are two notable projects within the city, one a school complex, the other an architect's office, both by Livio Vacchini. In 1970 Vacchini won a competition for the design of a new school in a late-1950s subdivision to the south of the city center. Construction was carried out in two stages between 1971 and 1974, and in 1979 a gymnasium was added to the complex. The organization of the school is reminiscent of Shadrach Woods' Berlin Free University plan, albeit only within a single level. The plan allows for all classrooms to have direct access to the outside, sharing common garden areas. Its tartan grid establishes a hierarchy of circulation and services separating the classrooms along one direction, and classrooms, circulation, and garden in the other. Hierarchically, the vaulted walks and the vegetation form the primary structures, placing the actual classrooms in the background. This prevents the school from becoming a monumental work.

The gymnasium follows a similar formal organization to the school segments, but here the perimeter zone of circulation spaces surrounds the central gymnasium floor. The extensions of the spines become stairs or toilets, and the zones between these form the entry loggias from north and

south, while those to the east and west house the administrative offices and specialized spaces. Because the gymnasium floor is below ground, the glass walls that one approaches through the loggias are in reality clerestory windows for the central volume. Additional light is provided by skylights outlining a square at forty-five degrees to the axes of the building. The structure consists of reinforced concrete with prefabricated elements. The two segments of the school and the gymnasium are askew to each other, since each responds directly to the geometry of its immediate surroundings. Together, these three discrete elements create a tension reminiscent of the plan for the Villa Hadriana in Tivoli.

In designing his new office building, completed in 1985 and located in the center of Locarno, Livio Vacchini saw the opportunity to explore the formal relationship between functions and their architectonic expression within a building. There is an anthropomorphic relationship between the three stories of the building and the particular function of each. The bottom floor connects the building with the city, while the work place is located in the middle, and the archives are on the top. The

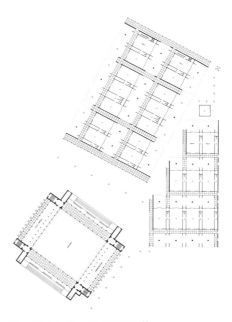

Scuole e palestra comunali Saleggi
View of the court area, elementary school
Ground floor plan

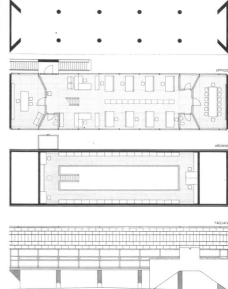

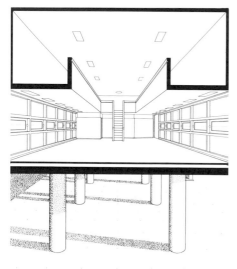

ground level is kept open, except for two end walls, the stairs that lead to the entry, and four pairs of columns; it is used for parking. The main level includes a large central drafting area with a private office and a conference room at either end; both are double volumes. Above, the archives overlook the central space. The structure is reinforced concrete. The end walls support the roof and an upper story of two structural bridges, while the middle floor is supported by the pairs of columns. This allows for an uninterrupted main work space awash with natural light from both sides.

Atelier Vacchini
Above left: View from Via Bramantino
Middle left: Interior view
Bottom left: Sectional perspective
Above right: Plans and elevations

Minusio, Brione s/Minusio, Orselina and Val Verzasca

Negozio Costantini
*View of the east corner,
with the front to the right*

Among a few older buildings and the predictable and ubiquitous new constructions on the hills above Locarno, there are three projects by Luigi Snozzi which merit attention. The first is the Costantini commercial building of 1977–79, in reality an addition to an older traditional structure. It is on a triangular site on the main road leading from Minusio to the hills above Locarno, and as is typical of buildings by Snozzi, the building is constructed in reinforced concrete, with a very pure geometry. As a result of the slope parallel to the road, the main level housing the commercial spaces is entered from one end, and is above the level that houses the carport and storage spaces. This is reached from the opposite side. The pure form of this wedge contrasts with the more fragmented forms of the older structures adjacent to it.

Further above and overlooking Lago Maggiore, two houses explore Luigi Snozzi's theme of "routes and limits."[4] The Kalmann House in Brione s/Minusio is the first of his single family structures investigating the theme of path between gate and object. It is also the first of his structures to study the notion of building perpendicular to the slope of the land, so as to afford a view beyond and simul-

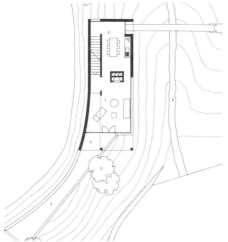

Casa Kalmann
Main floor plan
Interior view from the stairs
View from the street

taneously permit the view from behind. Its cast-in-place concrete structure is very Corbusian in resolution, yet is clearly resolved to address issues presented by the site: the living space in the middle level opens itself to the view by virtue of the curvature of the retaining wall on its west side. The quasi-open plan of the public level gives way to a regular and clearly compartmentalized layout of the private level above, although there is a measure of inter-connection between the living space and the master bedroom above by way of a balcony. Snozzi's second house on the hillside is the Bianchetti House of 1975–77, located near Orselina. It is reached through a gate that defines the parking area, across a bridge, and into the multi-level primary volume within the house. In a manner similar to the Kalmann House, Snozzi organizes the spaces within the Bianchetti House against the retaining wall to the west. It is here that the vertical circulation occurs. The south and east glass walls open to the view of Locarno below, and Lago Maggiore beyond.

The road that leads north to the Val Verzasca, away from Lago Maggiore and along the east shore of Lago di Vogorno, leads to the very traditional

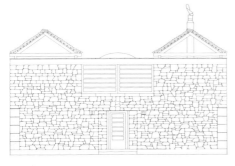

mountain villages of Corippo, Lavertezzo, and Brione/Verzasca. The chestnut covered hillsides are now sites for vacation retreats that overlook this manmade lake. Due to restrictive regulations that oversee new construction in areas deemed of historic character, Livio Vacchini was forced to allude to a *rustici* that had once been found on the site in his design for the Rezzonico House in Vogorno (1985). The vacation home is located among traditional structures in the San Bartolomeo area of town, but even from a distance one perceives that a transformation of traditional house forms has taken place. Though the gable roof seems like that of the surrounding buildings, it is clear that this is a house with a flat roof, and above it are two gable roofs of granite slabs. Vacchini has responded to the building restrictions by sheathing the concrete house with native stone. Its proportions, orientation, and appearance are sympathetic and even respectful of the surroundings. Livio Vacchini states his displeasure with the restrictiveness quite clearly, however: the house is an atrium house, an urban building type forced to disguise itself as a rural one. He writes:

If the regulations impose on me the use of construction elements that are technically inadequate... I use them only as an indispensable part of my architectural composition... [such as the] two stone roofs that do not keep out the rain.... If the regulations impose on me a style, I do it with great pleasure as a parody....[5]

Losone and Ascona

9.1 Scuola media cantonale 1973–75
Via Saleggi, Ascona
tel. (093) 35-75-51
Livio Vacchini and Aurelio Galfetti
Open during the academic year; visitors should ask for permission at the school office. Grounds are open and accessible year-round.

9.2 Casa Perucchi 1985-1986
Via Reslina, Losone
Franco and Paolo Moro
Private; house is visible from the road.

9.3 Casa Fumagalli 1985
Via delle Quercie, Ascona
Livio Vacchini
Private.

Scuola media cantonale
General view and site plan

Losone is one of two contiguous communities across the Maggia river from Locarno. The other is Ascona, which occupies the low area that is formed by the deposits brought down the mountains by the river's waters. Losone is to the north and upstream, on the foothills. The cantonal high school complex by Livio Vacchini with Aurelio Galfetti (1973–75) in Losone is composed of two elements: one housing the academic spaces, and the second a gymnasium. The first is a square that is bisected axially so that four L-shaped, three-story structures define an atrium. These function independently from one another, each with specific classrooms on ground level, all classrooms and language labs above, and the large lecture rooms and individual rooms on the top. There was to be a dining hall, not built, in the form of a bisected square. Its design would have been the inverse of the geometry of the classroom complex: the dining hall would have been in the central square. The structure of the built sections is steel, with infill panels and glass block walls. The columns and beams of the classroom wings are painted red, while those of the gymnasium are violet and yellow.

A single-family house by the Moro brothers is located in the northern confines of a new subdivision in Losone. The Perucchi House (1985–86) is a pure rectangular volume in brick with a protruding loggia/portico on the south and topped by an arch roof sheathed in metal and painted sky blue. The composition has a larger solid penetrated by a smaller and lighter one. The plan follows the formal geometry established by this interlocking. Entry is on center through the service zone on the narrow east end, which also includes the stairwell and a toilet; the balancing space to the north is formed by the kitchen area, which is separated from the combination living/dining space by a counter. A chimney is located on the north wall, on the axis of sym-

metry. The upstairs has three rooms
opening to the loggia, with the stairs
and bathrooms forming the ends of the
service and access spine. As with other
houses by the Moro brothers, there is a
dialogue established between elements
based on a very consistent and clear
use of materials: concrete block for the
bearing walls and wood frames for the
openings. The windows and doors are
always set along the inside plane of the
volume, permitting the volume to read
as a primary solid that is carved to expose another volume of another
material.

In a recent suburban neighborhood
of Ascona, Livio Vacchini has
designed a magnificent house, a classical villa that at the same time is purely
modernist. The rectangular and highly
symmetrical plan of the Fumagalli
House places the various primary functions within a square on two floors,
with balconies surrounding three sides
of the house. On the fourth side are the
services—entry, baths, laundry, storage,
and stairs. On the ground floor are
found the living spaces, each divisible
from the other by sliding wall-parti-
tions. One half of the plan square is a
living/dining space; the other is further

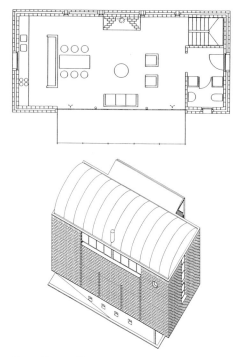

Casa Perucchi
View of the south side
First floor plan
Axonometric

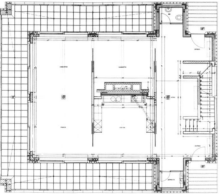

Casa Fumagalli
Exterior view; the main façade faces left
Main floor plan

divided into two, with the kitchen separated from a sitting area by the fireplace. Upstairs, a central corridor leads from the hall to the balcony, with the master bedroom, studio, and main bathroom on one side, the four bedrooms opposite. Sited on a carpet of grass, the concrete frame of the residence is sheathed in two sizes of white block. The lower volume of the structure reads as a carved solid with only the corners left intact, the floor of the *piano nobile* indicated by a thick granite band. The upper floor protrudes above and is set within, above the perimeter of the lower one. Materials in the interior are exposed concrete and wood, except for the large granite slabs that make the wall of the fireplace.

Verscio, Cavigliano, and the Valle Maggia

In one of the valleys west and north of Locarno are the contiguous villages of Verscio and Cavigliano overlooking the plain of the Melezza river and the Centovalli beyond. Both villages have so far retained a large number of their traditional buildings—although many are no longer used for their original purposes and instead are second homes—as well as some noteworthy contemporary insertions by Luigi Snozzi and the Moro brothers, among others.

The 1966 Snider House in Verscio is the result of the collaboration between Snozzi and Livio Vacchini. The new structure completes a complex with two older buildings to form a courtyard complex with the *rustico* and two houses (old and new), creating a *casa a ringhiera*,[6] a building type found in the area. The new structure is on the north-south axis, its west façade nearly completely blank. The new house indicates an affinity to the old constructions, with its plain stuccoed masonry walls reflecting the plain nature of the traditional structures. Its plan is

Casa Snider
View from above the courtyard
Ground floor plan

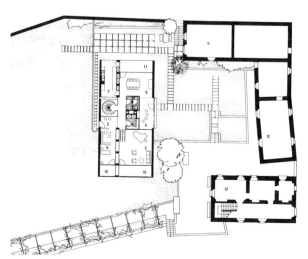

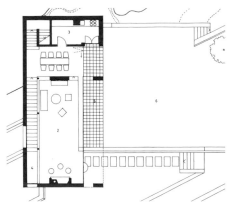

Casa Cavalli
Interior view along the stairs
Main floor plan

organized in two parallel zones separated by a row of columns, with a perpendicular tri-partite division. The narrower western half houses the entry, kitchen, and two of the sleeping areas, with the center section housing the vertical circulation and other services. The ground floor houses all the group spaces, the upper story all the individual ones. A basement houses the technical services.

The Cavalli House, also by Snozzi, is located immediately to the northwest of the Snider House. Its typology is similar, though its relation to the site is defined by the slope of the site to the north and its arrangement along a path that leads west from one of the small piazzas of the town. The Cavalli House is the first of the Snozzi projects that explores the idea of "routes and limits."[7] The main entrance is in line with the path, and is strongly defined by the overhanging solids of the upper stories. At ground level are located the technical services. The stairs leading to the main floors are against the west side of the house, and all the supports

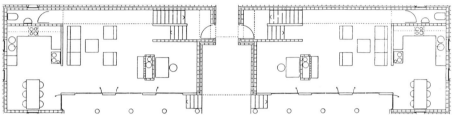

Two-family house, Verscio
View of the south elevation
Floor plan

Single-family house, Cavigliano
View of the south elevation

are located against the north wall. The main level of the house includes the family spaces and opens to the garden towards town. Above are located the sleeping areas and a work space. These spaces also face to the east.

A two-family house by Franco and Paolo Moro and built in 1981–82 is located on the eastern edge of Verscio, sited parallel to the road. The building faces south, and its two units are placed symmetrically about the perpen-

dicular axis. The entry, stairs, kitchen, and bathrooms are located along the north wall, allowing each living space and bedroom the view toward the valley. Typologically it is the transformation of the double-house type to form what in the United States is known as a "dog-trot" house. The main spaces face south to the garden. A technological insertion is the group of solar collectors on the roof.

In the adjacent town of Cavigliano is a single family residence, also by the Moro brothers. This small house is located among the new parcels north and uphill from the town. As with other Moro projects, the clarity of concept results from an economy of materials used: the exterior volume is made of concrete block, while all that is within and which can be seen through the perforations is in wood; the gambrel roof is covered with ceramic clay tiles. From the south, the house appears to be a granite block with a giant keyhole portico carved in its middle that houses a terrace and balcony. The plan reflects this, as all the spaces in the two main

Casa Sartori: *View from the road*

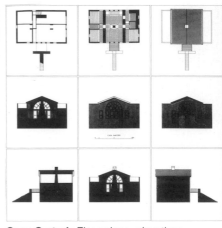

Casa Sartori: *Floor plans, elevations, and section*

floors are organized forming a C that faces this southern opening. Against the north wall in the center segment of the volume are all the services. On one side are the kitchen and eating areas below, two children's bedrooms above, and on the other, living space below, master bedroom above. The attic space has five skylights aligned with the keyhole and is finished as a studio. The base of the structure houses the mechanical and storage spaces, as well as an emergency shelter. Just to the east is the Flütsch House (1981–82) by Rody Roduner, a small structure above the road. Its atrium house plan is sliced in half along the diagonal to expose an open space. In Roduner's project, the result is a truncated triangular plan that presents the city two nearly blank walls each with a single shed roof turned inward to the pergola balcony.

In Riveo, along the Valley Maggia northwest of Locarno, a house by Bruno Reichlin and Fabio Reinhart, the Sartori House of 1979, presents a marked contrast to the projects by the Moro brothers or Snozzi. The Sartori House is in the Palladian tradition, a structure based on a nine-square plan with a gabled central section. Toward the road and the garden, the abstracted and transformed temple front—with its semicircular clerestory window above four elongated openings—gives a clue as to the interior. The *piano nobili*, in a manner consistent with its classical prototype, is raised above the ground and reached on axis from the garden façade. The road façade, on the other hand, is altered to respond to the placement of the house close to the property line. Inside, the central room of the single story house is a high-volume space. The secondary spaces are distributed to either side, under a lower roof. A hearth is placed in the center of the house. The architecture of the Sartori House reflects a search by Reichlin and Reinhart for solutions based on more diverse cultural roots than that offered by autochthonous rural structures of the region. It is a search that results in structures that are more attuned to the traditional urban architecture of the region, where painted stucco façades are common, and to the more universal model of the villa.

Mezzovico and Torricella

11.1 Casa Spinedi 1982–83
North of the town center, Mezzovico
Franco and Paolo Moro
Private; house is visible from adjacent streets.

11.2 Casa Hohl-Gabutti and Casa Pasquini 1983–84 and 1984–86
North of the town center, Mezzovico
Remo Leuzinger
Private; the two houses are located in the same area as the Spinedi House.

11.3 Casa Tonini 1972–74
South of town center, Torricella
Bruno Reichlin and Fabio Reinhart
Private.

As with other settlements that are located near the major highways that connect the cities of the canton Ticino, Mezzovico, the adjacent town of Vira, and nearby Torricella to the south have become bedroom communities with a number of interesting single-family houses. In Mezzovico in particular, structures by the Moro brothers, Remo Leuzinger, and others present the opportunity to compare and evaluate current house design. These structures are found in the new subdivisions between the two towns.

The Spinedi House by Franco and Paolo Moro (1982–83) is sited perpendicularly to the slope of the land, an orientation that permits the primary spaces to face south, with the entry and all the circulation spaces along the north wall. The floor plan is a simple rectangle: a basement that includes the mechanical and storage spaces, together with the required emergency shelter, and a main floor having the kitchen and eating spaces separated from the living space by a freestanding element that includes the chimney and a half bath. In concept the building is a gabled volume that is surrounded by a larger but lower perimeter volume—a two floor balcony on the south and the stairs and entry element on the north. The balcony element is an abstract hexastyle portico that gives access to the terrace at ground level. While these elements on either side of the body of the house are left unpainted, the principal volume is painted pale blue. A seamed metal roof covers the structure.

Two houses by Leuzinger are located near the Spinedi House. Both have a traditional distribution of interior spaces. The Casa Hohl-Gabutti (1983–84) and Casa Pasquini (1984–86) present an interesting contrast to the one designed by the Moro brothers. Leuzinger's designs reflect his years of appren-

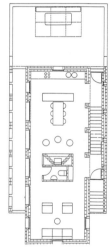

Casa Spinedi
View of the portico
Main floor plan

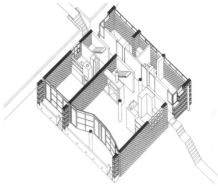

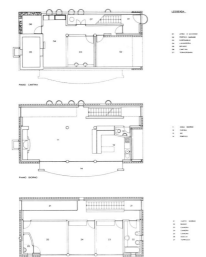

Casa Pasquini
The house from the southeast and axonometric

Casa Hohl-Gabutti
View from the south and floor plans

ticeship with Botta. The Hohl-Gabutti House is a rectilinear volume defined as two segments that are given definition by the use of two different colors of modular concrete blocks. The monochromatic principal volume includes the living spaces of the house and is finished with a red block. The gray and red service portion, with its vertical glazing, includes the halls and stairs. The symmetrical articulation of the principal façade is further formalized with a protruding, reinforced concrete porch. It is at the two ends that the portions of the total structure are visible. The two-family Pasquini House is based, in contrast, on a nine square plan which is primarily solid along three sides and open to the south. This façade is a three bay brises-soleil loggia which indicates the location of the two units, to the left and right of a concrete block fin. As with the Hohl House, the two-family house is built of concrete blocks, and the two color banding is used to accentuate the loggia.

Also nearby are two residences by Gianfranco Richina and Roberto Sedili and the school by Pietro Boschetti and Franco R. Boretti. The houses by Richina-Sedili are new structures that present a contrast to the others discussed above. The Gabutti House, adjacent to those by Leuzinger, and the Zocchi House, to the south of these, reflect an attitude about design based

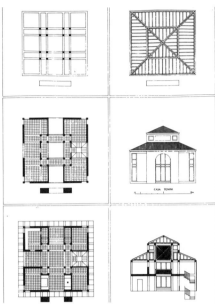

on the use of planar and chromatic elements to articulate surfaces. The middle school was completed in 1973 on split levels that follow the slope of the site. The plan is organized about a linear spine with classrooms on the top two floors, entry, offices, and common spaces in the middle, and gymnasium below.

The Tonini House in Torricella has enjoyed very deserved notoriety since its initial publication. Its very clear Palladian planning owes more to Aldo Rossi's analogical design principles than to the regional building types, yet in the manner in which it attaches to the land and in its use of materials, it is clearly of the place. Reichlin and Reinhart have organized the plan about a central rotunda which in this modest interpretation is the central square of a nine-square composition. The entry, circulation, and secondary spaces are located axially to the high volume of the central space—its Josef Hoffmann dining set is the centerpiece of the house—while the other major spaces are located at the corners. A traditional disposition of rooms places the living

Casa Tonini
View of the entrance elevation
Plans and elevations

spaces on the ground floor and the private ones above overlooking the central area. There is a clear identification of the diverse construction elements. The structure is reinforced concrete with interior wood partitions, metal window frames, and railings.

At the old center of the village of Torricella, there is also a very modest renovation of an existing *rustici* by Gianfranco Richina and Roberto Sedili. These architects add a new entry and services element to the Brughelli House on the upper floor and regulate the principal façade to the east.

Origlio

Casa Polloni
View of the main façade
Interior view
Floor plans

Origlio has attracted an interesting cross-section of projects that provide habitation within a fairly mundane setting of suburban subdivisions. The Polloni House of 1980–81 by Mario Campi, Franco Pessina, and Niki Piazzoli is located in a newly suburbanized area south of the town proper, along the banks of a lake. The division of the land is regular, between parallel access lanes. The house begins from this perspective, but detaches itself from its free-standing neighbors by reinterpreting a different archetype. Here Campi-Pessina-Piazzoli transform the courtyard or atrium house by reversing the relationship between solid and void: it is the "solid" of the garden that defines the "void" of the house. The design is also based on two parallel volumes, one the entry gate and the other the house proper, both highly formal in their compositions. The house begins as an apparently symmetrical exploration which then shifts to local symmetrical compositions. The symmetrical entry pavilion is aligned with the middle upright of a composition of four square openings on the facing façade of the house, three large ones and the fourth divided into four small squares.

However, the entry axis is off-center to the real axis of symmetry of the façade, which is indicated by the middle upright of the subdivided square. This shift in plan is created by the diagonal glass wall of the living room. The central openings of the façade are complemented to the right by three vertical openings with a circle above, which corresponds to the center point of the mullions that are formed by the four small squares. The interior of the house is resolved about the central entry space, a two-story volume that extends from outside to inside the house. Terminating the axis of symmetry are the stairs to the upper floor. The structure is reinforced concrete and masonry block which are covered with stucco; metal frames are used for windows and doors, while the interior floors are polished marble.

Sited on a hillside in the Carnago area of Origlio, the Togni House by Emilio Bernegger, Bruno Keller, and Edy Quaglia (1979–81) is a rectangular masonry solid with two interior levels that place the living spaces on the floor above the sleeping rooms, thus permitting a view beyond, from the main spaces of the house towards the valley. The lower floor is arranged with a hallway that connects an entry and double volume study to the stairs leading above. The upper floor overlooks

Casa Togni
View of the south elevation
Interior view

the lower hallway and study, with the living and eating areas flowing together with the kitchen. Construction is typically in concrete block, with small square windows punctuating the bedroom and bath areas and a band window that becomes the study window\wall completing the form. The top edge of the walls are articulated with a course of alternating colored blocks laid vertically. A second house by Ber-

Casa Delorenzi:
View of the south elevation
Axonometric

negger-Keller-Quaglia, also completed in 1981, is found elsewhere in Origlio. It is made of two equilateral legs of an L plan, with diagonal exterior stairs located on the outside corner of the structure, facing a parking lot downhill from the house.

The Delorenzi House of 1982 by Mario Botta, also in the Carnago area of Origlio, is part of the architect's thematic exploration of nine-square plans. Here the volumetric interpretation results in a solid lifted by two oversized cylinders and a slab from the surrounding ground. Within the circular elements are located the technical services at ground level and two niches off of the living space. The cylinders become cubic sleeping alcoves on the second floor above the ground, while through the floors the north third of the overall volume encloses the entry, stair, kitchen, and bathrooms. The purity of the form and the clearly contemporary architecture is apparent, yet so is its analogical relationship to the traditional *rustici*, such as the one found on an adjacent lot. Botta's expected elements—the use of gray concrete modular block, the presence of slot or cleft windows on center that become square openings at their bottom, and the use of pediment transformed into a vaulted skylight—are all present in this project.

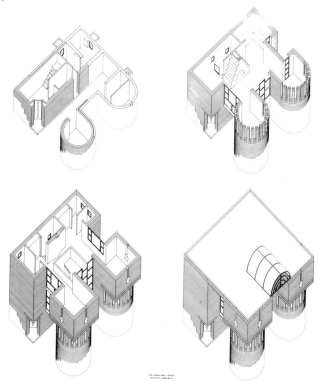

Tesserete, Bigorio, Cagiallo and Vaglio

Casa ripozo anziani
View from the garden

The towns of Tesserete, Bigorio, Cagiallo, and Vaglio are located in the central valley north of Lugano. Their closeness to the city makes them highly desirable sites for residence: Bigorio in particular affords dramatic hillside views of the valley and city beyond.

The residential building for the elderly by Luca Bellinelli, dating from 1976–78, is one of two structures by this architect in Tesserete. The other is the school complex of 1979–84, on the north edge of the center of town. Both are reinforced concrete structures and of very clear geometry. The residential building consists of a four-story slab at the end of a small cul-de-sac. The structure is raised on *pilotis*, creating loggias along the two long sides. The one facing north, enclosed by glass, forms the entry into the building and provides access to the ground floor community functions; a triangular stair and elevator tower gives access to the upper floors. The other, left open, provides a covered walk along the south-facing garden side of the building. The individual efficiency apartments in the upper floors fit between the structural bays and also face south. The Tesserete school complex consists of two rectilinear structures forming an **L** in plan. The longer leg consists of five repetitive modules that house the various classroom spaces. The shorter leg encloses the assembly rooms.

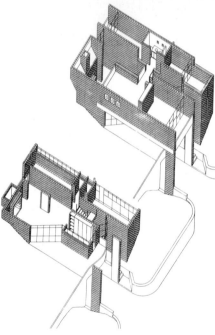

Casa Hunziker
View from above looking east
Interior view of the living spaces
Axonometric

On the road that leads north of Tesserete, just beyond the edge of town, Rudy Hunziker built his house and studio. Dating from 1979–80, the structure marks the beginning of his professional career. The house is sited on a hillside perpendicular to the road and is formed by two rectilinear masonry volumes that are connected by the glass house of the stairwell and hall. The element to the north houses the bathrooms, studio, and guest rooms, while the one to the south contains the living and bedroom spaces. The lower level of the south block is divided by a diagonal glass wall that forms an exterior covered terrace opposite the living spaces. A double volume connects the space by the fireplace with the upstairs sitting area. The construction materials, concrete masonry blocks and cast-in-place concrete, are left exposed and contrast with the painted metal frame of the windows and doors. Hunziker also designed a pair of four story apartment buildings (1981–82) behind the former train station of Tesserete.

Martin Wagner designed a two-family house on a hillside below the center of Bigorio, overlooking the town of Sala Capriasca. The 1978–79 structure combines direct gain and active solar elements to provide the water and air heating for the house. The two units are entered from above, from either side of a landing that becomes a greenhouse below. A central core runs the length of the building and is terminated

by the individual stairs; the solar collectors and storage tanks are located on the roof above the core. The building mass against the hillside to the north of the core includes the bathrooms and other services. Principal spaces of the dwelling units face south. The design is such that the structure could ostensibly be extended to the west along the hill. It is reported that the alternative energy systems cost one fifth that of conventional oil heating.[8]

The Clementi House in the Almatro area of Cagiallo was built in 1980–81. Designed by Remo Leuzinger, the structure includes two dwelling units within interlocking elements, one parallel to the road, the other slightly below the first and falling downhill. Leuzinger makes use of the grade change to define the private outdoor space behind and below the house. Inside, the larger unit occupies both

Two-family solar house, Bigorio
South-facing elevation and detail of the winter garden
Upper floor plan

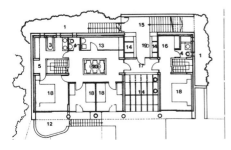

wings of the upper floor, with the sleeping rooms on the wing parallel to the road and the living spaces on the one perpendicular. Below, a small two-bedroom unit occupies the perpendicular wing, while the other wing includes an all-purpose space for the main dwelling. The structure is reinforced concrete and modular masonry unit with interior plaster walls.

71

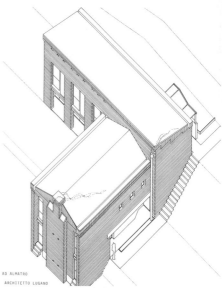

AD ALMATRO
ARCHITETTO LUGANO

Casa Bifamiliare Clementi
Exterior view
Axonometric
Interior view: the living area

72

Gianfranco Richina and Roberto Sedili designed the Sedili/Bernasconi House in 1985 in the center of Cagiallo. This symmetrical two-family house follows a different aesthetic, one tied to the tradition of painted façades. The single entry into this two-family house, indicated by an abstract pediment, gives the dwelling the presence of a large single-family structure. From the garden side, the two units are apparent. Because of the site that slopes down from the front street, Richina and Sedili have placed the bedroom areas of each unit half a floor above the entry, with the living spaces half a floor down so as to open to the terrace. The central area of the units includes the kitchen, halls, and bathrooms. Facing south on both floors are most of the primary spaces.

The Horat House by Rudy Hunziker, located to the north of the town center of Vaglio, dates from 1980–81. Originally on the edge of town, it is surrounded today by new developments that include a research station. The placement of the structure responds to the site in terms of both its location and its orientation, so that the primary views and the windows face west, south, and east, with the north façade entirely closed. In plan, the house resembles a T with a bulbous projection. This projection permits the living space of the ground floor to extend beyond the body of the structure and thus creates a covered terrace below. On the second floor, the bedrooms open onto the terrace that is created by the protrusion. The upstairs hallway overlooks the two-volume section of the living space that faces the hearth, a very articulated solid that is expressed both internally and on the exterior. The structure is reinforced concrete and modular masonry blocks. The façade is given some articulation by the use of two colors of block that differentiate the monolithic main body of the house from the stripped projection.

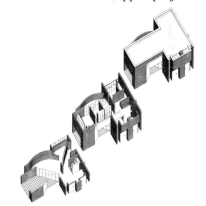

Left: **Casa Sedili/Bernasconi**
View from the street and view of the fireplace

Right: **Casa Horat**
The house from the southeast and axonometric

Sonvico and Cadro

Museo della Città
View of the press room
Interior axonometric

The partnership of Antonio Bassi, Giovanni Gherra, and Dario Galimberti executed its very first work, a small service structure, on the yard of a house just outside of Sonvico. Fittingly, it is here that one finds two additional projects. The first is the renovation and conversion of an old pressing mill, where walnut oil was produced, into a city museum that preserves the ancient press. The renovation was begun in 1979 and completed in 1983. Apart from restoring the structure, the architects created an oval entry space where displays can be exhibited and constructed a balcony in the main room where the press is housed. The press itself is imposing, a giant screw press known as Piedmontese *torchio*. The main trunk, which provides the balanced weight for the pressing mechanism, is chestnut wood with an inscribed date of 1582 that measures ten meters in length and weighs some 5000 kilograms.

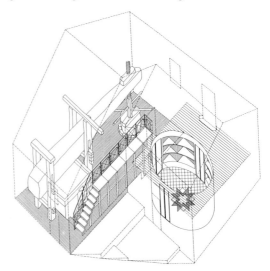

The other structure by Bassi-Gherra-Galimberti is the 1981 two-family house for the Malfanti brothers. The Malfanti House is on a relatively flat site on the hillside below the town center, with its principal view downhill and to the south. The structure is symmetrical, with the entry to both units from a central portico on the street side of the building. On the ground floor, the entries, kitchens, toilets, and stairs are located on this side. Upstairs, the two smaller bedrooms face north while the master bedroom of each of the units is given a corner of the structure. A two-volume section of the living space connects with the upstairs hall that leads to the balcony. As with their other residences, Bassi-Gherra-Galimberti are concerned with the definition of the exterior façade through the exploration of subtle changes in the plane, articulating the corner pilasters by minute changes of surface and by the use of changes of color. The design, moreover, is based on neoclassical notions of architectural form rather than autochthonous precedents found in the immediate area.

In contrast, a number of structures in Cadro illustrate the contrasting approach followed by Rudy Hunziker, Remo Leuzinger, and the partnership of Sergio Grignoli and Attilio Panzeri. Their architecture investigates more abstract notions of form: whereas Bassi

Casa Malfanti
View from the garden
East elevation

et al. clearly design houses that are based on archetypal forms, the projects in Cadro analogically transform the structural characteristics of the traditional, rural constructions in Ticino.

The first project, a complex of seven row houses designed by Hunziker in 1982–86, is located on the southwestern edge of Cadro and across from the town cemetery. Each unit has a front entry garden facing the common parking lot and rear yard towards the west. These identical dwellings have their circulation spines against the north wall. This spine is articulated by a continuous skylight above. Inside, a typical distribution of spaces is fol-

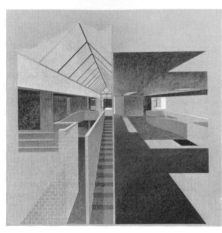

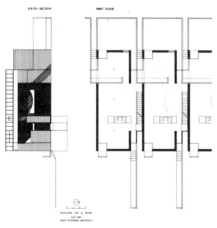

Row houses, Cadro
View of the entrance side
Perspective rendering of the central spine
First floor plan and south section

lowed, with living, dining, and kitchen below, and two bedrooms and a bathroom above. However, a spatial connection exists between downstairs and above through a cutout that pulls away from the straight run of the stair. Construction is in reinforced concrete and concrete masonry blocks.

To the west of these, across the cantonal highway and near the elementary school of Cadro, is the two-family Piffaretti House by Remo Leuzinger. Constructed 1983–85, the house is fundamentally a solid concrete cube that is sliced along the diagonal to create a simplified reinforced concrete loggia and expose a glass wall that faces to the view south and west. As with his other structures, Leuzinger uses concrete block and an exposed concrete frame for the building, while the large window wall and other frames are of metal painted black.

Also nearby, in the Cossio section of Cadro, is the combination house and photography studio Paltrinieri. This project by Sergio Grignoli and Attilio Panzeri from 1986 presents a stark contrast to the bland and banal structures built all around it, houses that range from quasi-traditional northern Swiss chalet look-alike, to those which escape description. Grignoli-Panzeri's design is a very cubic structure, of modular concrete masonry that alter-

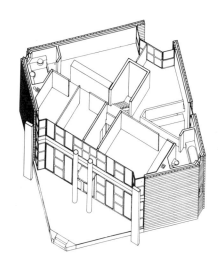

nates between three courses of gray and one course of pink blocks, with a free-form expansion on the upper floor that forms the service areas (stairs and bathroom). Otherwise, the dwelling is basically symmetrical about the short axis. The lower floor of the structure is occupied by the photography studio which fronts toward the cantonal road. The upper story comprises the house proper; it is accessible from the residential cul-de-sac parallel to the road.

Casa Bifamiliare Piffaretti
View of the south side and axonometric

Casa/Studio Paltrinieri
Views from the garden and the road

Lamone, Manno, Vezia and Arosio

15.1 Laboratory 1986
Via Cantonale, Ortarieta, Lamone
Pietro Boschetti
Open during regular business
hours; inquire at the office.

15.2 Geberit, S.A. 1982–84
Via Cantonale, Manno
tel. (091) 59-37-12
Claudio Pellegrini
Open during business hours: Monday to Friday, 9–12, 14–18.

15.3 Studio Hunziker 1983
Via San Gottardo, 9, Vezia
tel. (091) 56-63-22
Rudy Hunziker
The architect's office.

15.4 Single-family house 1969
Arosio di sotto
Tita Carloni
Private.

15.5 Casa Maggi 1980–81
Arosio di sopra
Mario Campi, Franco Pessina, and
Niki Piazzoli
Private.

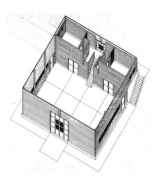

Laboratory
*View facing the
superhighway and
axonometric*

A number of new industrial and commercial buildings are located in the outskirts north of Lugano, along the Bellinzona-Chiasso super-highway. Three in particular are of interest, two based on nine square plans, the other a variation of the theme. The first is a small industrial structure by Pietro Boschetti to the south of Lamone and adjacent to the super-highway. The square plan has sixteen modules, with the overall proportions of the volume 1:3:3. A skylight runs on axis down the length of the building, providing natural light to the entrance and the work space, and serving as the unifying element with the two main doors. The entry, offices, storage, staff services, and mechanical equipment room occupy the northern fourth of the building in two stories, with the rest of the volume occupied by the actual work space. Conceptually the building is a stone structure within a metal one. The building is bright yellow, while the two square entry doors, the window frames, and the skylight are bright red.

The second is the new training center of Geberit, S.A. by Claudio Pellegrini. Built in 1982–84 and located on Via Cantonale in Manno, the combination office and classroom building has a nine-square plan. It is a two story volume organized around a covered central space that includes a vertical "tower element" incorporating the various products of the company—plumbing fixtures—as its *impluvium*. The axial entry, to one side of which is the stair, leads to the atrium that gives access to the four teaching spaces. On the second story are found the offices organized around a central balcony. The structure is cast-in-place concrete with concrete block infill.

Finally, Rudy Hunziker has built a commercial structure to house his office and two other businesses. Located on the main street of Vezia, the Via San Gottardo, the building is a free-standing struc-

ture with a tri-partite façade that acts as a gate into the site. The façade is a variation of Botta's Pfäffli House in Viganello. Constructed in modular block and reinforced concrete, the gate-like front includes two volumes articulated with an alternating course of blocks to either side of the reinforced entrance element. Above, a three part space frame substitutes for a pediment. The offices are located to either side of the entry portico.

Two contrasting structures are found in Arosio, one a project that reflects the attitude in the 1960s of basing design on a regional interpretation of Wright's prairie-style architecture, the other a 1980s project that clearly respects the characteristics of the traditional architecture of the region without replicating its elements. The 1969 single-family house by Carloni is a prairie-style house in the true sense. Sited to the east and below the town center, it is stone mass that hugs the land and is crowned by a floating, low-slung hip roof. In plan, the mass that is visible from the road contains the circulation and service spaces; the living spaces are located in the lower floor, and sleeping spaces above. All opens

Geberit, S.A.
The main elevation

Studio Hunziker
Elevation facing Via San Gottardo

Single-family house, Arosio
View of the house from the west

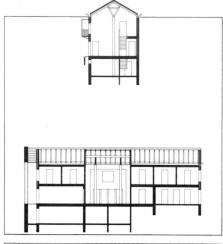

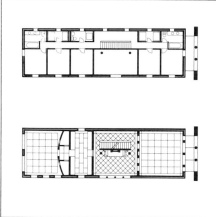

Casa Maggi
View of the temple front from the town center
View of the entrance side
Floor plans and sections

to the view to the south. The roof over-hang provides shade and cover for the terrace off the bedrooms. In contrast to it is the Maggi House by Campi, Pessina, and Piazzoli. The house dates from 1980–81 and is situated in the upper part of Arosio, on a site that overlooks the town center to the south. It is a traditional gabled structure of two stories with a garden to its west that is sited orthogonal to the slope of the site. The group spaces are located on the lower floor, and the sleeping areas are above, with the double-volume central living area the connecting element. When viewed from below, the house merges with its neighbors, its *in antis* temple front that faces the town center hiding the true nature of the structure behind a stone and concrete screen. The body of the house is detached from the screen front, connected only by the eaves of the roof and the terrace floor. An oversized cornice details the connection between roof and house body that is otherwise very pristine. Only a metal balcony and pergola attached to the west façade protrudes from the pure form.

Cureglia

Among a collection of new buildings located to the north of Lugano are structures by the partnership of Sergio Grignoli and Attilio Panzeri. Their work is characterized by the use of platonic volumes that are altered and recombined, always using the construction materials in lieu of any decorative elements on the façades. The first is the Tennis Club Cureglia, located to the north of the village center. The club house is a small linear building that terminates the axis established by five tennis courts. The structure, built in 1981–85, houses changing rooms to either side of a small café. It is built of modular concrete block with alternating gray and pink courses. A five-bay metal portico provides cover for the terrace that faces south towards the playing courts.

The other structures by Grignoli-Panzeri in Cureglia are two single-family houses, the Tamborini House (1979–81) and the Poma House (1980–82), and a group of semi-detached houses (1979–82). Together they illustrate the contrasting methodology within the approach followed by this partner-

Tennis Club Cureglia
View from the tennis courts
Interior view of the main space

ship. Whereas the design of the Tamborini House is based on a reductive transformation of a cube, the Poma House is based on two linear, interlocking forms. The Tamborini volume is eroded to reveal a terrace on one corner and carved to form the diagonal stair on the opposite side, and only a slab supporting the master bedroom's balcony protrudes beyond the perimeter. With the Poma House, the two volumes isolate specific functions of the house within two wings, with the principal living spaces located at the crossing. The semi-detached houses in a row are a response to the need for higher densities within the context of the traditional village, while retaining the qualities of the single family house. Thus, the solution followed by Grignoli-Panzeri gives each unit three exterior façades, and by displacing the volumes along a diagonal, each dwelling unit can have a clearly identified front entrance. The units have the services and stairs along the common walls.

Built during the same period, the house and studio Realini, located immediately to the north of the Poma-Taddei House, is a more complex project in its conception. Designed by Rudy Hunziker, this project follows a similar ap-

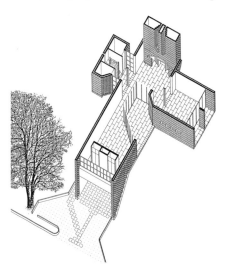

Casa Poma-Taddei
Left: Axonometric
Top: Exterior

Casa Tamborini
Middle: Exterior from the south
Bottom: Detail view of the terrace

proach to those previously discussed. However, the project by Hunziker is more of an investigation of architectonic elements rather than a transformation of platonic solids. The house can be seen as a combination of a thick wall and a volume that are joined by a glass roof. The "thick wall" part of the structure is linear in organization, beginning with the garage and followed by the studio—more properly a medical office—and other functions secondary to those principal spaces for family living. The other section of the house includes the living room, dining room, library, and television room below, with the master bedroom suite above. On the other side of the glass fissure, as part of the wall element, are the children's bedrooms and bath. The side elevation of the Poma-Taddei House recalls details from Louis Kahn's Ahmedabad project, particularly in the support of the shallow brick arch by a concrete spring beam. In the Poma House, the result is a somewhat anthropomorphic axially symmetrical façade.

Row Houses, Cureglia
View of the principal elevations

Casa/Studio Realini
View from the street and axonometric

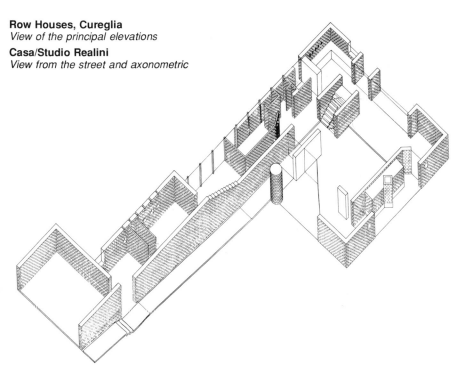

Lugano

17.1 Centro Macconi, S.A. 1974–77
Via Pretorio, 13
tel. (091) 23-94-44
Livio Vacchini and Alberto Tibiletti
The department store is open during regular commercial hours.

17.2 Comercio Ransila I, S.A. 1981–85
Via Pretorio, 9/Corso Pestalozzi, Lugano
Mario Botta
The various stores at ground level are open during regular business hours.

17.3 Banca del Gottardo a Lugano 1982–87
Viale Stefano Franscini, Lugano
Mario Botta
The bank's headquarters; public spaces accessible during business hours.

17.4 Library of the Convento dei Cappuccini 1976–83
Salita dei Fratti, 4/Via San Gottardo, Lugano
tel. (091) 23-91-88
Mario Botta
The library is open W–F, 14–17, and Sa 9–12, closed for vacation during August.

17.5 Casa Felder 1978–80
Via Antonio Riva, 9 Lugano
Mario Campi, Franco Pessina, and Niki Piazzoli
Private.

Comercio Ransila
Corner view, with the side facing Via Pretorio to the right

The largest and arguably the most important city in the canton, Lugano has always enjoyed great prosperity. It is a city with a population of some 30,000 in a metropolitan area with a population of about 70,000. Sited on the northern shore of its namesake lake, the city is a commercial and banking center as well as a tourist resort town, and in this manner is differentiated from the other major cities of the canton, Locarno and Bellinzona. Its relatively low elevation (under 1000 feet above sea level) means that within sight of the high Alps a Mediterranean climate and subtropical vegetation are found. While the historic center of the city lies on a flat area on the edge of the lake, the dramatic views from the adjacent hills and mountains give it notoriety.

Because the broadly based prosperity and growth enjoyed by Lugano has been mostly unaffected by the impatience of tourist-oriented commercialism, new commercial, educational, cultural, and residential structures in the city and surrounding towns include some of the more important projects built in Switzerland during the last fifteen or twenty years.

Along Via Pretorio, near the center of town, there are two adjacent commercial buildings, the Centro Macconi by Livio Vacchini and Alberto Tibiletti of 1974–77 and Mario Botta's recent Commercio Ransila I (1981–85). While in many respects these are rather sedate explorations, they are nonetheless ex-

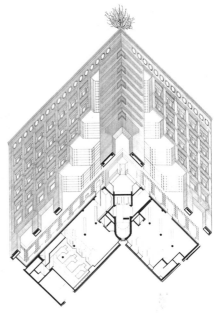

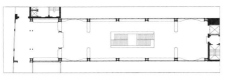

Left: **Centro Macconi**
Exterior
Ground floor plan

Above: **Comercio Ransila**
Axonometric

cellent solutions to the problem of building in a high density area, where commercial necessities dictate particularly efficient and succinct solutions. Vacchini and Tibiletti's building for the Macconi department store has a narrow street front, but the long façades face toward two courtyards. The steel structure is immaculately detailed. The steel, marble, and glass front façade of the seven story building is defined by two piers on the corners that are formed by parallel steel, wide flange sections. The division of the front is punctuated by cross beam reveals every two stories, with the two story base and one story attic reveal further indicated by square medallions at the intersection of beam and columns. The building continues the arcade along the street, while the upper floors between base and attic have

solid infill panels on either side of window walls.

The Ransila I office building by Botta is located on the corner of Via Pretorio and Corso Pestalozzi. Botta's building presents two mirror façades which merge at the corner. The building appears as a solid yet eroding brick volume near the corner, leaving only a massive pier to support the upper story and a solitary roof-top tree punctuating the corner. Revealed within is a steel and glass structure housing the commercial functions. The building forms an **L** in plan, enclosing a service court. The structure is reinforced concrete with brick infill defining the façades in the Lombardian romanesque tradition. This building elegantly resolves the problem of constructing on an urban corner, yet does not indicate a hierarchical differentiation between the two

85

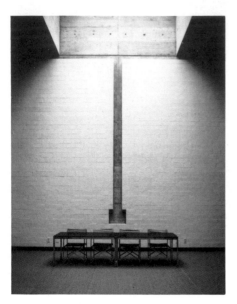

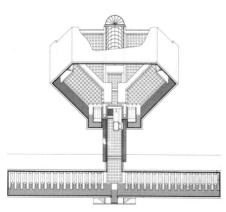

streets or between east and south orientation. A second phase, Ransila II, is currently under development and will occupy the site to the west of the existing building.

Botta also executed the large headquarters building for the Banca del Gottardo in Lugano along Viale Stefano Franscini across from the Villa Saroli (1982–87). The project is composed of four nearly identical segments linked together by a continuous element along the back. The four bodies extend to the edge of the site and give the impression of four detached structures rather than the typical urban condition of buildings that form a continuous street wall. Since the Banca del Gottardo faces toward the Villa Saroli museum in the middle of a park, Botta opted for this solution. However, the four elements of the six-story building are rather massive towers with only the center sections carved away to reveal any openings, their façades finished in masonry block. Inside, the various bank departments are distributed along the four elements, separated from each other by vertical circulation nodes. In its diagram, the plan could be extended indefinitely by alternating cores and volumes. At ground level, however, the four are not equal, with each of the triangular plan spaces performing a specific function. The upper levels are typical office floors designed to permit variations in their layout.

The first project by Botta in Lugano, however, was the Library of the Convento dei Cappuccini on Salita

Banca del Gottardo a Lugano
Library of the Convento dei Cappuccini
Interior view: the reading room
Axonometric

Casa Felder
Interior view of the entrance hall, exterior from the north, and the central courtyard

dei Fratti, located near the train station. Designed and built in 1976–83, the project involved the insertion of a contemporary structure as part of a seventeenth century complex. Botta opted to place the new construction below the forecourt of the convent. Only a skylight protrudes above ground by the side of the church. Downhill and facing toward the city center, the building creates a low retaining wall facing a small vineyard. Entry is gained through the lower floor of an existing building. In plan, the library is composed of two volumes, one a truncated trapezoid that includes a two-volume reading area with the skylight above, and the other, a linear one-story closed-stacks area with a roof that serves as the entry terrace to the library.

The Felder House by Mario Campi, Franco Pessina, and Niki Piazzoli of 1978–80, overlooks the lake and center of the city from atop a hillside. The solution for this "serene, Platonic, beautifully proportioned villa"[9] is an atrium house reminiscent of the Palazzo Riva, located adjacent to the new structure. The Riva palace is a truncated courtyard house, more properly described as a C-plan. In the Felder

House, the two legs of the elongated C (now a U) define the plan square which is completed by a screen wall. The Campi-Pessina-Piazzoli solution follows the archetypical atrium house: they give the primary focus of the interior spaces to the enclosed atrium or courtyard through a transformed loggia. The living spaces and kitchen are located in the lower floor, together with the car park and a small bedroom and bath. Above, the parents' bedroom suite is located on one side, while the three children's rooms are opposite the courtyard. The connecting space overlooks the two story volume of the downstairs hall and forms a sitting area. The courtyard is paved to form a square, with the missing wing completed through the planting of trees, thereby establishing a dialogue between the exterior garden and the atrium.

Massagno and Porza

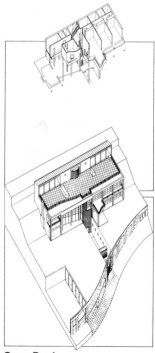

Casa Boni
View from the street
Axonometric

Massagno and Porza are affluent suburbs on the hills immediately to the north of Lugano, overlooking both the city and the lake. Among numerous very expensive but inconsequential residences, three of particular merit emerge, as does an interesting solution to the problem of building multifamily housing. A residential complex in the edge of Massagno at once satisfies the needs for the definition of the individual dwelling and a solution that responds to urbanistic concerns.

In the Tre Pini area of Massagno are two single-family residences by Mario Campi-Franco Pessina-Niki Piazzoli and by Mario Botta. Of the Boni House by Campi-Pessina-Piazzoli, Werner Seligmann states that it "can be understood as a commentary…on an archaeological, cavelike [sic] building and a modern space of frame, planes and volumes."[10] The house faces across Lugano toward the lake, as well as the hillside of Monte Brè and the suburban town of Viganello. On a steep site, the structure is a series of terraced elements, with the principal house a three-story slab building that is entered through a fissure in the bottom terrace. Within this terrace/podium are also located the garages, requisite shelter, guest rooms, keeper's apartment, and storage spaces. The front that faces the street is a rusticated wall clad in dark gray marble; behind and above this one catches a glimpse of a very pristine villa that Campi describes as "an homage to Terragni."[11] It is this dialogue between the base and the apparently freestanding house upon it that Seligmann refers to. Inside, all the service spaces are grouped against the back wall. The house is entered on axis one level below the main floor, and the void of the central stair separates the family spaces of the first living level

to either side on the first floor, and the parents' from the children's rooms on the second. The orthogonal structural grid of the house is altered by the curvilinear forms of the protruding balcony and the internal cubic, freestanding volume of the second floor study. This volume stands within the "*tour de force* of this house,"[12] the two-story space of the living room. The layered construction to the façade is reinforced by changes in the profile of the structural elements (square pillars on the outside and round columns inside) and variation of fenestration, from large panes of glass to glass block walls.

Mario Botta's Robbiani House is located on the same road in Massagno, designed and built between 1979 and 1981. A blunt, elongated cubical house punctuated by an oculus in the middle of its front façade, the Robbiani House, as with the house in Viganello, should be approached frontally, a perception only possible from an angled perspective (or when viewed from across the valley). In reality, the house is entered through a passageway indicated by a diagonal cutout on the far corner of the front. The oculus is a movable glass partition that retracts to expose the two-

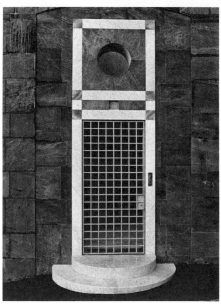

Casa Boni
Exterior facing the garden
Detail of the front entrance

story sun room directly to the exterior in summertime. The nearly symmetrical plan places a cylindrical stairwell with a triangular stair on axis. A hollow pier that serves as a portico on the lower level is on center within the volume and raises above as a two-story

Casa Robbiani
The house from the cul-de-sac
Axonometric

Row Housing, Massagno
View from Via Lepori
Axonometric

centering element topped by a triangular skylight. Otherwise, small variations distort the symmetry. On the main level of the house, the greenhouse "borrows" space from the dining room, while the living space includes a double volume that visually connects to the master bedroom above. In this second floor, the two children's bedrooms similarly extend into the volume of the greenhouse.

Also in Massagno, on a site that faces the intersection of two major roads, a project by Mario Campi and Franco Pessina provides a comparison between solutions for single-family housing in exclusive neighborhoods and those for multifamily housing in more conspicuous locations. The nine

Single-family house, Porza
View from the road and axonometric

row houses on Via Lepori, built in 1985–86, are designed to present a uniform façade which allows each three story unit to maintain a certain individual presence within the complex— a precedent found in the Rue de Rivoli in Paris, or Nash's Park Crescent in London, for example. The public orientation of the building is northeast towards Via San Gottardo, to which it presents a solid plane punctuated by groupings of square windows and tall, double-height portico openings. All the services of the units are placed against this wall. The opposite façade is faced by the units, and the façade reflects this. It is an ordered loggia in which each unit has a balcony above and covered terrace below, all facing the individual gardens that are terminated by pergolas. Parking for the complex is located below the gardens and is accessible from Via Lepori with the exit to the smaller Via Cabione. Each of the units, though small in size, benefit from a very straight forward layout. There are two types of units based on the two structural bay widths used, resulting in three wider central units than the groups of three on either side. The two end units, however, are further modifications, with the northwest-facing including a cylindrical glass protrusion capped by a cubic solid, and the south-facing unit expanded slightly. Each dwelling has a basement storage area and three floors above ground, as

well as a roof terrace. Overall, the imagery of the building is purely modernist, a ship with bow and stern and numerous smoke stacks.

The Moro brother's most recent house (1986) is located in a secluded cul-de-sac street in the adjacent suburban town of Porza. The plan of the house begins on the lower level as a square that inscribes a Greek cross along its diagonals. The legs perpendicular to the street form the entry spine and stairs, while the others include a shelter and storage area below and become the corner piers to support a truss above. The plan forms a triangle above, with the missing right triangle reflected by a paved terrace. Economy of space, as with other Moro designs, is the aim. This results in a very compact distribution of functions: the main floor is divided in two by the hearth and kitchen element, above which is located the single bathroom that separates master bedroom from children's alcove. The smallness of the interior spaces is mitigated by their geometry: they widen toward the glass wall created by the diagonal. Construction materials include exposed modular gray concrete blocks and reinforced concrete for the structure, a wood frame wall with window and solid panels, and a painted metal truss, fabricated of square tubing. Unfortunately, the original design was changed by the addition of two columns as center supports for what should be a structurally continuous truss.

Pregassona and Viganello

19.1 Casa Sampietro 1979
Via Arbostra, 27, Pregassona
Mario Botta
Private.

19.2 Casa Vanetta 1985–86
Via del Sole, 4, Pregassona
Remo Leuzinger
Private.

19.3 Apartment condominium 1986
Viganello
Sergio Grignoli and Attilio Panzeri
Private.

19.4 Casa Pfäffli 1980–81
Via Albonago, Viganello
Mario Botta
Private.

Casa Sampietro
View facing south

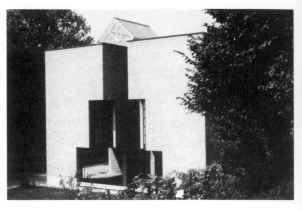

The towns of Pregassona and Viganello are to the east side of Lugano and across the small Cassarate river, on the side of Monte Brè. Projects by Botta, Bassi-Gherra-Galimberti, Grignoli-Panzeri, Leuzinger, and others are located in the newer subdivisions of both.

Pregassona, the northernmost of the two, is developed mostly on lower ground. In the Corte subdivision of the town, Mario Botta built an archetypal, cubic structure based on a nine-square plan, the symmetrical Sampietro House on Via Arbostra. Designed and built in 1979–80, the house is constructed of exposed modular concrete block. In plan, Botta divides the square into three parallel zones, two wide ones separated by the narrower circulation spine opening to the top of the house. The ground level of the structure is mostly open and contains the entry, laundry, and mechanical rooms. A kitchen/dining area occupies one corner of the main floor, with a studio space and completing this half. The living area faces a fireplace, which hides a toilet behind it. The top floor includes the master suite in one half and a second bedroom and bathroom in the other. The two sleeping areas gain a terrace from the cutout occurring in the middle third of the side wall. As a volume, the Sampietro House is a solid block carved on its two axes. The south wall has an increasingly smaller opening, and the east and west walls are equally divided from bottom to top, while the north wall has the protrusion of the bullnosed stairwell.

The Vanetta House by Remo Leuzinger is located on Via del Sole in Pregassona. Built in 1985–86, the project is an exploration on the transformation of a cube. What begins as an equilateral **L** on the bottom floor is added to so that by the third floor the house

forms a square with one-sixth of it removed along a diagonal. The walls following the orthogonal grid are built in gray concrete masonry, with the only course of pink masonry blocks on the top altering this. Along the diagonal, a different structure is revealed. The wall of the third floor alternates between gray and pink courses of block. A central column supports this diagonal bridge. The lower wall is cast-in-place concrete, with an undulating glass wall enclosing the middle level.

The apartment and office building by Sergio Grignoli and Attilio Panzeri in Viganello was completed in 1986. In this project, two identical towers are combined into a single structure in a continuation of formal design investigations by the architects. At ground level, the two entries lead from a central portico to the passenger elevators and stair towers accommodating each half of the building. Offices occupy the remainder of the floors. The upper floors include one floor of two-and-one-half room apartments, while the four floors above consist of duplex apartments. The lower duplex apartments have the living spaces on the lower floor and three bedrooms above. This is reversed in the upper duplexes, which also have access to private roof terraces.

On the road that leads up Monte Brè to the Albonago area of Viganello, another of Mario Botta's explorations is found. The Pfäffli House of 1980–81 is part of an exploration investigating the delineation of edges, as in the Rob-

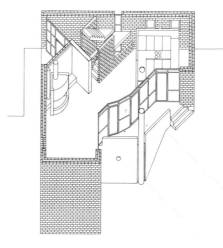

Casa Vanetta
Exterior of the south elevation
Interior: the living space
Axonometric of main spaces

biani House in Massagno across the valley. Unlike the earlier long, rectangular houses in Cadenazzo and Ligornetto, which are placed perpendicular to the slope in the first case and on a flat site in the other, the two structures outside Lugano are sited parallel to the contour of the slope, thereby commanding the view and at the same time establishing an edge. The house in Viganello is approached from a side path that leads to a stair on axis with the volume. Entry is gained through a vulvar opening into a covered area which includes the front door. In this house the interior stairs are not located on axis, but rather to one side, against

a corner. A triangular terrace covered by a glazed barrel vault is the central element of the *piano nobili* above the entry and storage level. As in the house in Massagno, this opening has movable glass partitions to make a winter garden in inclement weather. The main floor includes the living area on the same side as the stair, and the dining area against a wall, hiding the kitchen from view. The upper floor includes the master bedroom and bath, and a second bedroom and bathroom. The house backs into the hillside, attaching itself with a sinuous curve at the center of the retaining wall accentuated by a central skylight. The only real views are to the west, and similar to Botta's other projects, these views are controlled and accessible only through the central opening of the west façade. The house is constructed of modular concrete blocks, but what would be a very plain wall is given some articulation through the pattern created by rotating the blocks forty-five degrees. This visual interest also permits Botta to reinforce the axiality of the composition and the centrality of the barrel vault and winter garden.

Apartment condominium, Viganello
Street view

Casa Pfäffli
Right: exterior
Below: axonometric

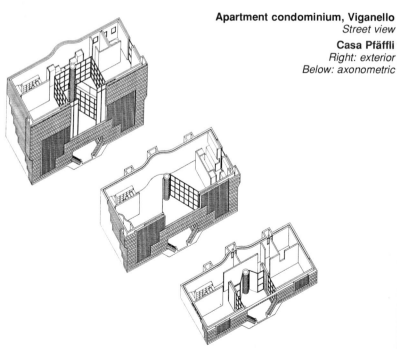

Muzzano, Breganzona and Sorengo

On the road leading up the hill to the town center of Muzzano, Via Ciustaretta, one finds a very interesting project by Emilio Bernegger, Bruno Keller, and Edy Quaglia: the Platis House of 1979–82. The house is a right triangle attached to a thick walled volume. Built of modular concrete block, the hypotenuse of the house opens to the view downhill and south from the structure. Five pairs of openings are located on center, separated by pillars and flanked by two slits with ocular windows above. Changes in coursing of the blocks along the edge of the roof create glyphs, and the exclusion of the corner block every eight courses implies quoined corners on this diagonal face. The slab behind is treated differently, with alternating color bands giving some semblance of symmetry to the northeast elevation. The house is entered at the lower level and is an open space within the triangle, with only the kitchen counter and four columns interrupting that space. The entry, stairs, and toilet room are contained within the slab. The floor above includes three bedrooms, two sitting areas, and two bathrooms; a cutout overlooks the fireplace.

Casa Platis
View from the east
View of the south façade
Main floor plan

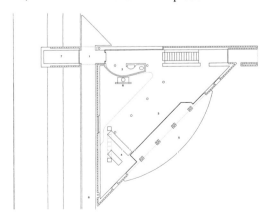

The nearby house for Dr. Huber by Claudio Pellegrini, dating from 1985, is located on Via Orbisana above Muzzano. This large, three-story house cascades down the hill, changing as it does from the asymmetrical volume of the upper pavilion to a very formal, two-story composition when viewed from the garden below. The house plan is developed within a rectilinear form, with a central cylindrical stair as the focus of the layout. Claudio Pellegrini very skillfully works the reinforced concrete structure to frame a central large opening with a protruding semicircular balcony, while the smaller side bays are punctuated by a large circular window above a small square one.

The Kress House in Breganzona is the most recent house by Mario Campi and Franco Pessina. The design continues their exploration of the courtyard typology adjusted to a sloping site, i.e. the main body of the house is placed against the high ground. The house is located in a typically small plot in a recent subdivision, where houses are by necessity built as close to the property line as permitted and thus in very close proximity to one another. As an axially symmetrical design distinguished by its compositional balance, the house responds to the impositions of the site by placing the service spaces, stairs, kitchen, bath-

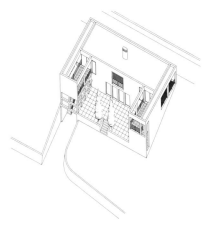

Casa Dr. Huber
View from the garden
Interior view

Casa Kress
View from Via Lucino
Axonometric

rooms, and storage against the slope, allowing all of the primary spaces to benefit from the view. Privacy in the courtyard is gained by the extension of two arms on either side of the main volume. The carport, main entry, and terraces are contained within.

Sergio Grignoli and Attilio Panzeri designed a cubic single-family house on Via alle Campagna in Sorengo (1983–84). The cube is sliced along a diagonal from the mid-points of the west and south sides, truncating the volume and revealing the central diagonal axis of the entry with the *de rigueur* vault skylight above. The plan of the house places the stairs on this diagonal axis, near the true center of the square, and locates the service spaces—baths and kitchen—in the area immediately behind. The structure is exposed modular block and cast-in-place concrete columns and floor slabs.

Single-family house, Sorengo
View from the Via alle Campagna
View from the garden

Montagnola, Carabbia and Vico Morcote

21.1 Scuola elementare consortile della Collina d'Oro 1981–84
Town center, Montagnola
tel. (091) 54-81-91
Livio Vacchini
Visitors should ask for permission to visit the buildings in the school office.

21.2 Casa Bersier 1980
Carabbia
Antonio Bassi, Giovanni Gherra, and Dario Galimberti
Private.

21.3 Villa SCI/ARC 1985–86
Town center
tel. (091) 69-12-87
Martin Wagner
The school is open Monday to Friday, 8–17; a café is located on the ground floor.

Scuola elementare consortile della Collina d'Oro
View of the main elevation from the town square
View of the courtyard

The project in Montagnola for the new Scuola elementare consortile della Collina d'Oro by Livio Vacchini began as the winning entry in a competition held in 1978. An atrium building, the school opens to the south in the upper story. The building is approached from the north, where it forms the town center that reflects the geometry of the Piazza dell' Campidoglio. Vacchini writes:

I have always associated the idea of a school with the presence of porches or galleries. This is the original source of the whole project. I have tried to work so as to make this school express the three things that a building may be by nature: a limit created in the middle of the landscape; a door which leads to a different world; and a place to be at ease in.[13]

The C-shaped main building houses the offices, library, auditorium, and shops on the ground level, and the classrooms above. The fourth side of the atrium houses the gymnasium, which has its main level below the courtyard. Its roof serves as an outdoor plaza from the classroom level, and it connects this to the hill beyond. The building is a very elegant, modernist structure of post-and-lintel frame in reinforced concrete and metal, with glass and marble infill facing the town square and wood and glass towards the atrium. The façade to the town square is a continuous surface, save for a thin ledge

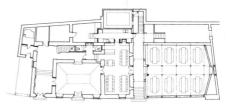

SECOND FLOOR

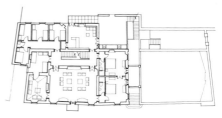

GROUND FLOOR

Casa Bersier
The house from the garden
Villa SCI/ARC
Top right: View from the terrace
View of a faculty room
Floor plans

at the bottom of the upstairs infill panels; however, it is not without articulation. A very elegant pattern is created by the bands of black and white marble veneer, together with the thin metal frame of the glazed infill.

In Carabbia, the Bersier House by Antonio Bassi, Giovanni Gherra, and Dario Galimberti (1980) forms part of the architects' exploration of neoclassicist themes in small, detached structures. The tripartite body of the house is centered about a double volume with single run stairs and chimney element. The living spaces on ground level and the private rooms above are to either side of the central space. The main orientation of the house is to the south view, facing a garden.

The renovated villa in Vico Morcote by Martin Wagner (1985–86) serves as the campus for the Southern California Institute of Architecture (SCI-ARC) program in Europe. The house is located adjacent to the village center and retains all of the characteristic elements of large residences in such settings; its interior has been transformed only where necessary. On ground level, the central hall leads to the stairwell; rooms straddling each side of the hall complete the composition. The room to the left offers a café opening to a terrace designed in the tradition of the Ticinese *grotto*. The classroom and sleeping rooms for students and guest faculty are contained on the upper level.

Malcantone

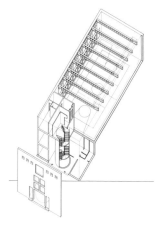

Palestra
View of the main façade from the road
Exploded axonometric view

Although Malcantone might appear to be removed from all activity since it is the isolated corner of the Ticino, its closeness to Lugano has meant that it, too, has seen marked growth. Important projects are found in this area of the canton, along the mountains between Lago Lugano and the Italian eastern shore of Lago Maggiore.

In Neggio, the new school gymnasium by Mario Campi, Franco Pessina, and Niki Piazzoli (1979–80) is a pure concrete box whose dimensions are based on the size of a basketball court. The building stands behind the Villa Soldati, where the classroom spaces are located, and is sited with its principal axis perpendicular to the slope of the land and facing west to the town itself. The main entrance to the gymnasium is through the west façade, entering into a rectangular lobby housing a cylinder within which are framed metal stairs on a triangular plan— an insertion of divergent geometries that is reminiscent of the main stairs of both Yale University galleries by Louis Kahn. The gymnasium floor is a two-story space lighted from the north by full-height windows, and from the south by a slit skylight along the plane of the wall. The lower level and a second story over the entry lobby contain the changing rooms, a smaller gymnasium, and offices.

In the town of Caslano, on the plain between Monte Mondini and Lake Lugano, there is an earlier

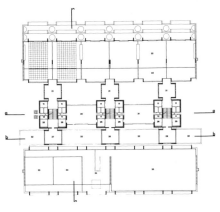

elementary school by Campi-Pessina-Piazzoli (1972–73). It is located in a recent subdivision on an orthogonal site. The school is divided into three classroom sections. Its further division into "servant" and "served" spaces permits repetitive elements allowing the structure to conceivably be extended *ad infinitum*. Pairs of classrooms on two levels are reached from the common spaces by way of circulation towers containing the services.

Scuole consortili
Detail of the east façade
Floor plan
View of the entrance lobby

The Trentin House by Emilio Bernegger, Bruno Keller, and Edy Quaglia (1982) is located in the same general area. This very sculptural, cubic composition in modular concrete block is situated among other suburban houses and apartment buildings. Its design

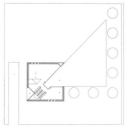

Casa Trentin
Views of the exterior and stairwell
Floor plan
Casa Bellini
The house from the road

On the upper floor the structure is further carved, with a triangular terrace accessible from the master bedroom. A third floor studio also has an exterior terrace, this one over the second bedroom below. The volume of the building is completed by a fin on the southwest corner which supports the cross beam of the top edge. The exterior decorations result from the alternating courses of masonry on the overall shell, from its contrast with the metal frame and glass of the large window walls within the volume, and from the play of shadows cast by the freestanding fin and overhead beam on the wall surfaces.

The Bellini House (1978) is located in Monteggio, at the furthest confines of Ticino and adjacent to the Italian frontier. It is the first project by Antonio Bassi, Giovanni Gherra, and Dario Galimberti. Unlike their more recent work, this project reflects the autochthonous architecture of the region, particularly that found in the higher elevations, where wooden balconies are typically attached to the structure along the long side, and where houses are entered on the upper floor. Here the living spaces are above the private areas of the house.

clarity, striking profile, and detail of construction make it stand out among its neighbors. The cube is dissected by a central diagonal. The entry and stairs are placed on either side of the diagonal which separates the eating and kitchen area from the living space; the living space opens to an exterior triangular court which extends beyond the perimeter of the structure into the garden.

Rovio and Riva San Vitale

Casa Della Torre
*View from the south
showing the main volume
View from the southeast*

The drive to Rovio leads up from Melano, on the federal road between Lugano and Mendrisio. Situated on Monte Santa Agata, Rovio is a perfect site from which to view the lake valley below and the Mendrisiotto beyond. Rovio is also the hometown of Tita Carloni, and it is here where two of his older projects are located: the "zig-zag" house of 1957 and an adjacent single-family house of 1968, both situated near the small, seventeenth century chapel of San Vigilio.

To the north of the center of town, two more recently built projects are worth mention. First is the Della Torre House by Emilio Bernegger, Bruno Keller, and Edy Quaglia of 1979. This house has an L-shaped plan which faces south and east to the center of town in the foreground and Lake Lugano and Monte Generoso beyond. The main body of the house is parallel to the hill. The bathroom is placed above the kitchen and entry, and the sleeping spaces above an outdoor covered area, while in the perpendicular wing only the double-volume living room and the stair are enclosed.

Tita Carloni's most recent work, designed with his wife Julia Carloni, is their own house. Completed in 1986, the house clearly reflects recent trends in Ticinese architecture: a central opening to

Casa Carloni
The main elevation facing the road
View from above

an otherwise solid volume, the use of modular masonry units, and so forth; however, it is simply a continuation of the explorations which Carloni has always followed. This house especially illustrates his preoccupation with the region's building traditions, traditions found nearby in the chapel of San Vigilio and other small country chapels and parish churches. In the Carloni house, the solidity of exterior masonry structure implies a certain construction

crudeness, albeit very refined in execution. It gives way to a very pristine and rich interior. The only obvious entrance faces the road. This semi-circular orifice is notched to permit entry on an axis leading from the street to the interior cylindrical volume of the stair. Within the opening, glass walls on either side of the cylinder complete the trapezoidal court, and beyond one can see the interior spaces of the house. The compact house is sited against the side of the hill. It is built of conventional bricks and has a truncated T-plan.

Across and near the shore of the lake's head, the community of Riva San Vitale has also benefited from its very talented resident architects. Among these are Flora Ruchat-Roncati, Ivo Trümpy, and Giancarlo Durisch. Each has been involved in the design of school buildings for the town. The earliest projects are the complex of elementary and maternity schools (Aurelio Galfetti, Flora Ruchat-Roncati, and Ivo Trümpy: the elementary school buildings of 1963–64, 1970–72, and the maternity school of 1968), and the gymnasium (Flora Ruchat-Roncati and Ivo Trümpy, 1973). The most recent of the schools is the middle school by Durisch. Completed in 1982,

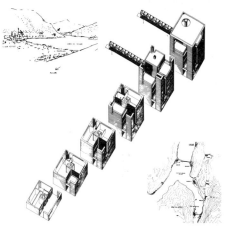

the building is a variation of the traditional atrium building. Of cast-in-place concrete construction, the four nearly identical wings of classrooms are separated from the central atrium by a very abstract loggia. The central volume is further delineated by the forty-five degree rotation of its coffered ceiling; the remaining triangular roof sections are perforated by circular skylights.

Two houses in Riva San Vitale merit attention, one by Mario Botta, and the other by Giancarlo Durisch. First is the Bianchi "tower" House by

Scuola media cantonale
View from the south

Casa Bianchi
View of the house and axonometrics

Botta (1971–73), located to the north of the center of town, off a lakeside road on the slopes of Monte San Giorgio. The house is oriented to the view across Lake Lugano, facing directly toward Monte Generoso, and is entered across a bridge on the upper level. Botta distributes the various functions

Casa/Studio Durisch
View from the municipal parking lot

of the house on four levels, each of
which also combines a terrace that allows ample opportunity to view the
landscape from indoors as well as from
the outside. The square plan is divided
asymmetrically. An interior tower, also
square in plan, houses the stairs connecting the various levels. From the exterior, and especially from across the
lake, the massive corners and flat roof
make this rather small structure appear
monumental.

The other house in Riva San Vitale
is Durisch's own house and studio/of-
fice (1973–74). Visible from the parking area near the center of town, the
Durisch House and Studio shares
Botta's design predilection for clear
volumes. In this case two identical
right triangles face each other to form a
court in the middle. Two free-standing
walls complete the court. The two right-
triangular volumes are solid concrete
walls along their outside legs, while
their hypothenuses are glass walls
screened by concrete *brises-soleil*.

Ligornetto, Stabio and San Pietro/Stabio

Casa Induni
The entrance viewed from the drive

The towns and villages of the Mendrisiotto enjoy a less hilly topography than other areas of the Ticino. Near the border with Italy, towns such as Ligornetto and Stabio offer the advantages of small town living while providing the convenience of access to the superhighway connecting Switzerland with Milan and the industrial regions of northern Italy. In this general area, both Mario Botta and Ivano Gianola have built a number of laudable works. Gianola has followed a design methodology which explores the craft of building, encompassing the whole structure and the most minute element of the interior of a house, such as in the recently completed renovation of a farm complex to serve as a design institute, the Casa Tognano in Coldrerio. There are also exceptional works of postwar architecture in the area, period pieces in the International Style and Frank Lloyd Wright's 'prairie architecture.'

In Ligornetto, for example, an early house by Tita Carloni with Luigi Camenisch is among the best examples of the Ticinese "prairie style" architecture. The Induni House predates the house in Arosio. It is situated on the west edge of town where the hills begin, in a lot secluded from view by the topography and vegetation. The house is entered along a long portico on its north side. The upper and main level of the house includes the bedrooms on one side and the living spaces on the opposite, all open to a south-facing terrace which is covered by the low hip roof. Below, an additional bedroom and studio open to the garden.

Mario Botta's Bianchi House offers a very different solution. The building is located on the opposite side of Ligornetto and is conceived to form the edge of the agglomeration. Designed and built in 1975–76, the house is a rectangular box very much

like the house in Cadenazzo, although its disposition on the site is quite different and its construction is based on a different notion. Here Botta opens the house on the longitudinal sides, with the primary views facing west toward the town center. The views are controlled by a central slit. On the exterior the façade is banded with alternating courses of gray and pink masonry units, alluding to a decorative tradition in the area, as found in some of the older structures in the center of Mendrisio, the funerary monuments in the local cemetery of Balerna, and on a house in the center of Morbio Superiore restored by Ivano Gianola.

To the southwest of Ligornetto is Stabio and its adjacent suburb of San Pietro. Stabio is located next to the Italian border, and so a few warehousing and industrial concerns are located there as well. Stabio developed around the base of a small hill that rises some thirty meters above the valley floor; the adjacent natural springs led to the building of a spa in the town. There are a number of recent projects in Stabio and San Pietro di Stabio which illustrate the range of design directions typical of the Ticino in general and the Sotto Ceneri region in particular. Included among its newer institutional buildings

Casa Bianchi
View from the west
Scuole elementari
View of a classroom building
View of the entrance from the south

are a school and municipal offices complex by Tita Carloni (1972–74), a home for the elderly by Claudio Pellegrini, and the new Raiffeisen bank building by architects Lino Della Casa, Luigi Pellegrini, Francesco Rapelli, and Marco Rossinelli, completed in 1987.

The school and municipal offices complex is developed on a sloping site near where the road to the suburb of San Pietro di Stabio breaks away from the cantonal road to Ligornetto. The buildings are characterized by their saw-tooth roofs with north-facing skylights. Classrooms are raised above common areas and offices, and their supporting columns help to define the public areas and give protection from inclement weather. The parallel classroom buildings are supplemented by secondary structures housing ancillary facilities. The structure is reinforced concrete and has a stucco exterior.

Located on Via Montalbano south of the school, the San Filomena home for the elderly (1983–85) is located on a suburban site surrounded by single-family houses. Designed by Claudio Pellegrini in 1979–80 for the Fondazione Pietro e Giulia Realini, the four-story structure provides both staff facilities and specialized services for the elderly who reside in its forty one units. Offices, dining hall, kitchen facilities, chapel, and social center—a small café—occupy the ground level. The typical floor has three sections of efficiency apartments arranged around a central core of stairs, elevator, staff areas, and storage rooms. A small common area protrudes towards the street. Located by the circulation core, it serves as a day area for each floor's residents. Besides the required shelter, the basement houses facilities normally associated with a home for the elderly, such as dis-

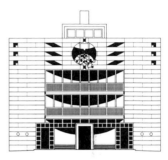

Casa per anziani S. Filomena
Exterior and typical floor plan (top)

Cassa Raiffeisen
Main elevation and ground floor plan (lower left)

pensary, emergency medical rooms, and a morgue. Construction is reinforced concrete and modular concrete block. The façades to the sides and garden are articulated by the deep recesses of the apartment balconies, while the side toward the street is a symmetrical composition centered by the triangular projection of the common areas, below which is the main entrance. This central portico-like element is framed with a giant concrete portal, flanked by blank concrete block walls.

The recently completed Raiffeisen bank building (1985–87) by Lino Della Casa, Luigi Pellegrini, Francesco Rapelli, and Marco Rossinelli is located to the east, on the cantonal road to Ligornetto. The new bank building, a mixed use structure which houses apartments above the banking levels, is a biaxially symmetrical cubic structure. The façades are decorated by alternat-

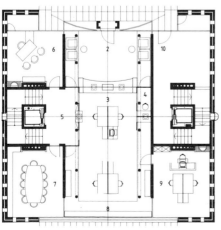

ing stripes of white and gray. Each side of the building is divided into horizontal thirds. The lower part of the façades facing the road and the backyard is also divided into thirds vertically. The central third of the front façade at ground level is a recessed curved wall; a portal indicates the entry to the bank lobby, while a doorway on the left leads to the elevator lobby for the upstairs apartments. This is balanced by a similar treatment on the opposite side, which is the bank manager's office. Two balconies are above, and the top level is punctuated by a circular cutout on axis with the portal below. The plan of the building begins with an irregular nine-square grid. On the axis perpendicular to the entrance, the tellers' desks occupy the center space; the stairs to either side of the center space each encase a small elevator. One set is within the banking space and leads to the basement vault and bank storage areas. The stair leading above gives access to the two apartments per floor.

Stabio is best known, however, for its houses. Lino Della Casa is owner of the 1965–67 house in Stabio by Mario Botta, a very Corbusian structure raised on *pilotis*, with a protruding stair diagonal to the body of the structure. Besides the house by Botta for Della Casa, three houses best represent the new constructions in the town. The most published of these is the "Casa Rotonda," the Medici House by Botta. Subject of a monograph and illustrated in nearly every book on recent architecture, the Medici House is an anomaly among a very bland and disparate collection of suburban houses to the north

Casa Medici
View from the south
Axonometrics

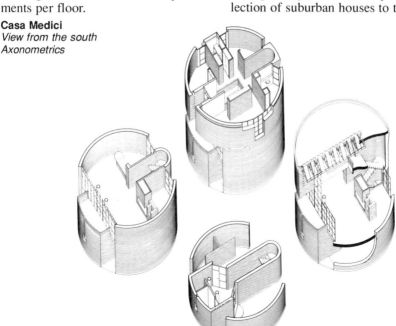

of town. Next to the vine covered hills on the border with Italy, it stands defiantly in this neighborhood, its views tightly controlled by a limited number of openings. The house dates from 1980–82, and is part of Botta's exploration of the placement of a unitary object on the landscape, not unlike his exploration in Pregassona or in the tower house in Riva San Vitale. As in each of these cases, Botta is exploring how to arrange and enclose rather typical spaces within a pure volume and symmetrically about a central axis. This central axis also serves as the vertical and horizontal spine, with the living spaces of the dwellings distributed to either side. The house is on three levels: the entry, services, and parking are on ground level; the living, dining, and kitchen are above, with the private spaces placed at the top.

In contrast, the architecture of Francesco Rapelli, as expressed in his own house, is a slick interpretation of an Art Deco aesthetic, more suited to the neoclassical architecture of the cities than to the autochthonous structures of the region. The Rapelli House of 1985–86 is a highly symmetrical structure, entered on either side of the central stair. The first floor above ground level includes two one-bedroom flats organized around central living spaces which share a common terrace. The top floor is devoted to the Rapelli apartment, also organized about a central living space, with the bedrooms and kitchen

Casa Naef
View from the garden
Casa Rapelli (bottom)
Front elevation

on the corners of the house, and the stairs, bathrooms, and loggia on center with the two axes. In plan, curved elements are introduced to reinforce the principal axis: the stairs on the street side and the bulging projection of the loggia on the top floor. The roof of the house curves slightly along this main axis and is completed with flat sides.

A similar approach to the Medici house by Botta was taken by local architect Luigi Pellegrini in his own residence in San Pietro di Stabio. In 1962, he had built one of the very first houses that used exposed BSK modular concrete blocks on the façade, allowing the constructive qualities of the structural block to come forward without a mask of stucco. His more recent Naef House on Via Campagnola in San Pietro di Stabio was built in 1983. This very compact house has a square plan rotated forty-five degrees to the street. The ground floor houses the family spaces, with the sleeping rooms above. In this solution, the only internal elements are diagonal to the exterior wall, thereby maintaining the dialogue of rotation. While the architectural expression is purely contemporary, the constructive qualities of both the Medici and Naef Houses are attuned to the traditions of the rural architecture of the Ticino.

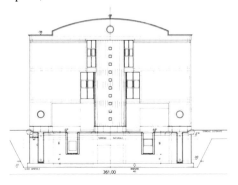

Balerna, Castel San Pietro and the Morbios

25.1 Palestra comunale 1976–78
East of the municipal cemetery,
Balerna
Mario Botta
Inquire in the office for hours when
the gymnasium may be visited.

25.2 Centro artigianale Crivelli e Cernecca S.A. 1977–79
Via delle Fornaci, Balerna
Mario Botta
The businesses housed in this
complex are open during regular
hours.

25.3 Centro "Saima" 1982–87
Industrial zone, Balerna
Franco and Paolo Moro
Inquire at the office.

25.4 Row houses, Quartiere Cereda 1974
Via delle Fornaci, 16c, San Antonio, Balerna
Tita Carloni, Lorenzo Denti, and
Fosco Moretti
Private.

25.5 Apartment building 1980–82
Via al Dosso, Balerna
Elio Ostinelli
Private.

25.6 Casa Bernasconi 1978–79
Via Prada, 20a, Balerna
Ivano Gianola
Private.

25.7 Casa Rusconi 1983–84
Via Obino, Castel San Pietro
Ivano Gianola
Private.

25.8 Two-Family House Crimella 1980
Corteglia, Castel San Pietro
Ivano Gianola
Private; fronts to a public street.

25.9 Scuola media e palestra 1972–77
Via Franscini, Morbio Inferiore
Mario Botta
Inquire in the school office.

25.10 Row houses 1984–86
San Simone, Morbio Inferiore
Antonio Bassi, Giovanni Gherra,
and Dario Galimberti
The exterior of the houses can be
seen from the street.

25.11 Casa Pusterla 1982–84
Town center, Morbio Superiore
Mario Botta
Private; house is visible from the
road leading to the center of town.

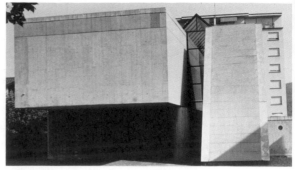

Palestra comunale: *The main elevation from the street*

Between Mendrisio and Chiasso lies the town of Balerna and its suburb of San Antonio. On the hillsides above are the towns of Castel San Pietro, to the west of the cascading Breggia River, and the two Morbios—Superiore and Inferiore—to the east. A number of interesting and important structures are found here, from workshops and schools to single-family houses.

In the center of Balerna, the community gymnasium (Palestra comunale) by Mario Botta (1976–78) is located next to the municipal schools and to the east of the cemetery. Botta's gymnasium resolves the problem of siting an athletic structure in the center of town, in a manner similar to how Snozzi designed the gymnasium in Monte Carasso. In both the scale of the building is diminished by utilizing the slope of the land and suppressing the gym floor below street level. In composition, the Balerna gymnasium is a slightly modified rectangular volume placed perpendicular to the street, barely wide enough to enclose a basketball court. It is dissected by a skylight and carved asymmetrically by a curved glass block wall to create an entry. The volume expands to one side to allow room for the stairs to the lowest floor. A linear skylight, placed off-axis, visually extends the entry to the back of the building. From the front, the reinforced concrete structure begins the dialogue between diverse solids. The major volume cantilevers above a glass block partition and is separated from the narrower, sloping volume of the stair by the skylight. A glass ribbon separates this volume from the protrusion of the secondary stairwell. As with other Botta buildings, the compositional concern for solids and voids is plainly apparent. Nearby, the maternity school by Ivano Gianola (1971–79) is next to the road leading to Morbio Inferiore.

The complex of workshops by Mario Botta, the 1977–79 Centro artigianale built for Crivelli e Cernecca S.A., is located to the south of town. Follow the road to the left of the train station under the tracks to the suburb of San Antonio. The complex is based on a nine-square grid, with the four corners formed by solid volumes which act as giant supports for a space-frame skylight over the central court. Three of the volumes are cubic, while Botta adjusts the fourth to the property line by curving its outside corner. In a manner similar to the articulation of his houses, Botta distributes the functions of the shops on three levels. Here the actual work spaces are in the bottom floor, administrative offices are in the middle, while residences are above. The two upper floors are differentiated from the base on the exterior of the complex by the carved center piece of the balcony. Construction is of modular concrete blocks and reinforced concrete. The steel structure of the skylight is covered with translucent plastic panels.

The recently completed warehouse and offices for the Saima company, which specializes in transporting cargo from Italy to the rest of Europe, was designed by Franco and Paolo Moro (1982–87). The location of this structure is clearly tied to this function. Sited on the city limits of Balerna, in an underdeveloped area behind the rail-

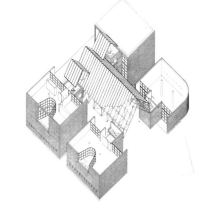

**Centro artigianale Crivelli
e Cernecca S.A.**
*View from behind the complex looking
south*
Axonometric

Centro SAIMA
View under construction

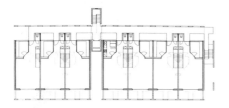

Row Houses, Quartiere Cereda
View from Monte San Antonio

Apartment building
View from the southwest
Lower floor plan

contain the stairs and services, and define an interior open space spanned by two great trusses. The office floor is supported between these trusses so that the podium base below remains as open space for the warehousing of products. Beneath this, the various support and technical spaces are found. The end blocks are constructed in reinforced concrete, with surface articulation from the form work accentuating the painted horizontal bands. There is a barrel skylight running longitudinally down the center of the middle portion of the building, and its width continues in the vertical slit down the center of the ends, where the entries and stairs are located.

In 1974, a group of row houses was constructed on Via delle Fornaci in the San Antonio area of Balerna, past the location of the Botta workshops. These houses of the Quartiere Cereda are by the group called the Collettivo di progettazione, 2, a joint venture of Tita Carloni, Lorenzo Denti, and Fosco Moretti. In their collective form, these row houses read as a continuous low-rise building which is punctuated on the roof by a series of triangular skylights. A dozen two-story dwelling units form the complex. Each unit contains three bedrooms above the living spaces, each with front and back gardens. The upper floor projects beyond the lower one, creating a covered and shaded path on the public side.

Another similar housing complex exists in Balerna, an apartment building on Via al Dosso by Elio Ostinelli. Built in 1980–82, the disposition of the building resembles the one by Carloni et al. Here, however, the building is four stories: the lower two floors consist of shops and commercial spaces, while duplex apartments, accessible from an exterior hallway, are above. This upper part is visually separated by a continuous screen which also protects the

road yards of Chiasso, the Saima building reflects the regional affinity for purity of volume and for dialogue between materials. In their design for this large structure, the Moro brothers allude to the great trussed bridges of the late eighteenth and early nineteenth century as a way of expressing the function of the structure and the company it houses. The solid block ends

upper floors from the west sun. The south façade also has a giant screen; this one conceals the exterior emergency stairs. The complex is painted a light yellow and is highly visible from the adjacent superhighway. In the case of this complex, the use of colors to delineate façade elements is in keeping with the baroque and neoclassical traditions of the area, rather than the autochthonous structures.

On Via Prada in Balerna, the Bernasconi House of 1978–79 by Ivano Gianola similarly reflects the multicolored aesthetic of the baroque and neoclassical periods, a tradition born in Lombardy and common in the Mendrisiotto. In this cubic design, Gianola articulates the two main façades differently. The entrance of the house is from the east. This checker-

Casa Bernasconi
View from the southwest of the garden side
View of the entrance side

Casa Rusconi
View from southeast facing Chiasso
View of end elevation

115

Casa Bifamiliare Crimella
View of front elevation
Floor plans

board façade, with its central door and band windows above, contrasts with the three stories of loggia on the opposite side. The middle level of the house includes the entry, bedrooms, and baths, while the upper floor is an undivided living area.

The Bernasconi House is the first of three houses by Gianola in this area of Ticino. Another structure, the Rusconi House in Castel San Pietro (1983–84), illustrates the divergent directions explored by this architect. In this case, a very rustic, two-story, rectilinear house has exterior rubble walls and a copper clad, shallow, barrel vaulted roof. Here the southern façade facing downhill is nearly solid, while the entry on the north includes a balcony above and is relatively formal in its composition.

The two-family Crimella House in Corteglia, Castel San Pietro (1980) is a project by Gianola akin to his house across from Bellinzona in Carasso. As with the Minotti House, the two-family structure in Corteglia is a traditional gabled structure, nearly symmetrical on both front and back. The two houses also have nearly identical plans. The variations occur in the division of the floors: one unit has two rooms below and above, the other has one large and one small room below, with three above. The stucco façades are seashell pink, except for the white outline of the entries. Green shutters close the side elevations' openings. The house is roofed with red tiles.

The middle school and gymnasium complex in Morbio Inferiore is among Mario Botta's best known projects. It is a highly controlled design that clearly delineates the edge of the town against the hillside. The design dates from 1972 and was completed in 1977. Three sections compose the complex: the school proper, the gymnasium, and a small house for the custodian. The gym and small building form the entry to the complex. Both are organized to provide a diagonal view of the school building, which is rotated thirty degrees to the orthogonal grid of the street and gym. The school is based on a repetitive module, each containing four general and two special class-

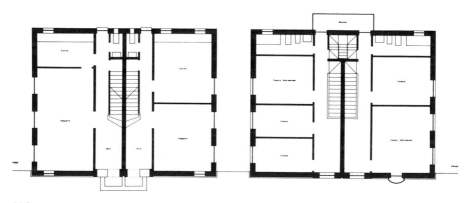

Scuola media e palestra
View of the entry court and sculpture: the school building is in the background

Scuola media e palestra
View from the northwest with the gymnasium in the background

rooms on the two floors above the ground level common spaces. Each module is based on a nine-square grid. A central spine runs longitudinally between the modules, while the classrooms and other primary spaces are positioned facing east and west. Giant rooftop monitors bring daylight to the circulation spine, while upper floor light shelves and deep recesses below provide some measure of sun control to the classrooms. The theme is varied at the south end of the school building. The two modules closest to the gymnasium have a wider void separating them, created by the principal stairs and elevator cores. An auditorium/cafeteria is located on the top floor of the end module, above the library. This module is adjacent to the gymnasium, separated by the amphitheater; thus, all the school-wide facilities are concentrated in one location. The complex is constructed in reinforced concrete with painted steel door and window frames.

Two sets of row houses by Antonio Bassi, Giovanni Gherra, and Dario Galimberti are located on the city limits of Morbio Inferiore, adjacent to Chiasso. Dating from 1984–86, the eight houses on two rows are archetypical contiguous structures, each with gable front and back, three stories high. The complex was constructed using federal housing subsidies, which in turn controlled the permitted spaces within the units and the type of construction. Even so, the architects have explored the use of a central high volume around which to place the spaces within the units. The exterior of the row houses reflects the architects' predilection for façade articulation through the use of subtle surface variations and changes of color. The pilaster corners are formed by a minimal differentiation of surface planes. The façades are identical for the two blocks, with differentiation occurring front and back: two versus three windows upstairs, and a circular attic window instead of two quarter circles.

Uphill in Morbio Superiore, the Pusterla House by Mario Botta (1982–84) overlooks the whole valley. Located adjacent to the road leading to town, this project is a variation of Botta's recurring theme of cubic, nine-square volume such as is found in the house in Pregassona, the one in Origlio, and the Casa Rotonda in Stabio. In the Pusterla House, however, there is a clear directionality to the structure, accentuated by the curved wall and the diagonal disposition of the face brick. The rotation of the brick in this manner allows the house to be "activated" by the setting sun. To intensify this effect, Botta had the concrete brick surfaces painted with metallic aluminum paint.

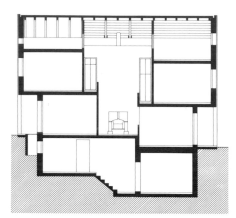

Row houses, Morbio Inferiore
View from the road
Longitudinal section through one unit

Casa Pusterla
View of main elevation facing west from the road
The entrance elevation and view to the west beyond

Chiasso and Environs

Chiasso is the border city with Italy. As the principal point of entry into Switzerland from the south, the areas near the highway interchange and the city's extensive railroad yards serve the freight industry. The hillsides above Chiasso have commanding views of the border terrain and are typically heavily developed with single-family houses of every description, while construction in the valley from Chiasso to Mendrisio has responded more to the industrial exigencies of the area.

Houses by Ivano Gianola and Elio Ostinelli are located among these new residential developments. The Ostinelli House by Gianola (1973) illustrates the architect's exploration of cubic construction in brick masonry. Located above Vacallo overlooking Chiasso, this house is organized into two parallel volumes displaced from each other. One serves as carport and entry, the other is the house itself. Entry is gained by going downstairs from the carport across a covered gap and into the house proper. The typical family spaces are within the entry level, including a double volume living area, with the two sleeping areas and baths above, and a roof terrace on top. Gianola's design explores certain Corbusian traits, such as the roof garden, in this highly inventive design, which make the Ostinelli house a welcomed relief to the topology of the subdivision.

Two houses by Elio Ostinelli are also found in Vacallo. Near the one by Gianola is the Guerrieri House. Designed in 1977, this house appears to be made up of two segments, in a manner similar to the nearby house by Gianola, and as with Gianola's, the Guerrieri House is made of brick. Its geometry, however, diverges from Gianola's. It is an extended single rectangular volume. A triangular volume is formed by a terrace and an exterior stairs leading from the parking area up to the entrance. Here Ostinelli places the living functions above the sleeping

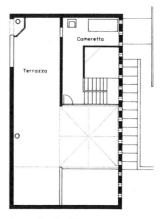

Casa Ostinelli
View from below
Section
Floor plan

rooms, thus improving what already is a magnificent view over the valley below. The exterior planes are carved by regular openings, again, in a manner similar to the house by Gianola.

The Hoderas House in the Cognuno area of Vacallo dates from 1975. It is also located among many contemporary but less successful single-family houses. In this case, Elio Ostinelli has kept all the functions within a rectangular volume. The only protrusions are the *brise-soleil* on the west façade. The traditional disposition of the plan does include a double volume living area.

On the right side of the road leading from Chiasso to Vacallo, adjacent to a small tennis club and across from a church, there is a large, apparently abandoned structure. This 1978–80 clinic was designed by Luca Bellinelli, with Elio Ostinelli as collaborator from 1979. The building is composed of two elements, the long slab of the rooms and technical services, and the rotated cube of the group spaces, including a restaurant, library, and other annexes. The clinic is still not open.

In 1984–85 Rudy Hunziker designed a single-family house in Pedrinate. Located just outside the

Casa Guerrieri
View from below and axonometric
Casa Hoderas
View from the west

southern edge of the town, this house is characterized by the stark contrast between the two brick façades forming the **L**-plan body of the house, and the *brise-soleil* of its third side. The brick walls are reminiscent of the house in Ligornetto by Mario Botta, as it shares with it the use of alternating color bands, in this case created by using three courses each of light and dark gray modular brick. The plan of this very small house is rather straight forward, the stairs and bathroom form one of the double walled brick sides, while the rest of the space is left rather open and permits views south. However, the resulting volume is much more complicated, resulting in a collage of forms.

Clinic, Vacallo
View from the south

Single-family house, Pedrinate
View of entrance and garden
View of back side

Brick walls are capped with concrete; a stair protrudes above the line of the east wall; the north wall is sliced by a vertical window which is transformed into a triangular skylight; the *brise-soleil* projects above the line of the brick sides. Inside, there is a volumetric connection between lower and upper floors. A bedroom and studio occupy the upper level; the hall leading to these serves also as an overlook to the loosely defined entry hallway.

South of Como

27.1 Cassa rurale e artigiana 1978–83
Via Provinziale, Alzate Brianza
Superstudio: Adolfo Natalini with
G. Frassinelli and F. Natalini
The bank is located north of the
town center. Public areas can be
visited during office hours.

27.2 Officine Meccaniche 1980–81
Sirone
Adalberto Caccia, Paolo Colombo,
Rita Mangone, Paolo Monti
Inquire at the office during regular
business hours.

Cassa rurale e artigiana
View from main parking area

Officine Meccaniche
Floor plans

The architectural culture in the Ticino has always looked south for direction, in particular towards the Como-Milan axis. This is particularly true during the present century. In particular, the architecture of Terragni in Como—and his Casa del Fascio in particular—is still highly influential with the current generation of architects, as is evident in the work of Mario Campi. But the current architectural climate in Como is less clear, less inspiring. There are, however, two structures which merit mention. They are the well documented rural bank building by Adolfo Natalini and Superstudio, located in Alzate Brianza, and a small addition and renovation to a factory in Sirone by Caccia-Colombo-Mangone-Monti.

The Rural and Artisans Savings Bank in Alzate Brianza is located to the north of the town center, less than an hour from Como on the road to Bergamo. Dating from 1978–83, this project by Adolfo Natalini of Superstudio with G. Frassinelli and Fabrizio Natalini combines "traditional and sophisticated techniques of construction, between the classical and vernacular idiom."[14] The bank building is located on a long and somewhat narrow site which, due to programmatic requirements, resulted in the diagonal placement of the structure to the roads.

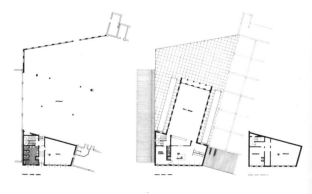

This structure and the computer center in Zola Pedrosa (BO), both by Natalini, share an overall structural concept based on exterior reinforced concrete structure straddling a nearly transparent parallelogram. Only the ends, which contain the stairs, elevators, and rest rooms, are solid. In between, the floors are divided according to need with no interruptions by vertical structural members. The ground level contains the general banking areas, with the middle level arranged along a central hall between the end spaces and a nearly identical upper floor, save for the large computer room at one end. Its very pure form is distorted by two major elements which protrude: a curving volume forming the main entry at ground level and the main meeting room above, and a house for the caretaker. The stone cladding of the savings bank, with its two-tone horizontal banding, reflects the traditional Romanesque of the region.

In 1980–81, the Milanese firm of Adalberto Caccia, Paolo Colombo, Rita Mangone, and Paolo Monti designed a

Officine Meccaniche
Exterior
View of the employees' dining hall

small addition and renovation for an industrial concern in Sirone. The project required a cafeteria for the employees as well as additional office spaces. Caccia-Colombo-Mangone-Monti use the new construction as a unifying element between two disparate existing structures, bridging industrial buildings of two different scales and on two different geometries with a neutral connecting element. The new building is characterized by repetitive perforations from the street. By placing the dining hall on the upper floor, above the additional work area, Caccia et al. have given the collective function of eating a clear ceremonial preeminence. The very sensitively proportioned rectangular hall is surrounded on three sides by window walls. One end opens to a loggia and roof terrace, the other contains the serving area. From the interior, this elevation is an abstract hexastyle temple.

The Valsassina

Casa per tre famiglie, Baiedo
View from below
Front elevation facing west

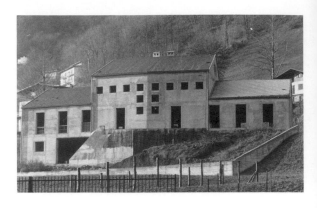

The valleys above and to the east of Lake Como form part of the transitional area between the mountain region and the river plain—the prealpini. As with other areas in the region which have remained somewhat isolated over time, the traditional architecture of the Valsassina has evolved into a clear, distinguishable series of prototypes. Not completely isolated from Lecco, the valleys in this area are increasingly desirable sites for second homes. It is in this area where much of the built work of Milanese architect Luca Scacchetti is found. He is conducting a very detailed investigation of the building typology in the Valsassina, so his own work is laden with references to this traditional architecture.

In Baiedo, two houses by Scacchetti are located side by side, on the road between the town and Pasturo. Begun in 1983, they are interesting transformations of the traditional rural structures in the area. Both are gabled structures, one a three-family house with a slight bend in the middle sited parallel to the slope of the land, the other, one-family, placed perpendicular to the site. These houses are particularly well proportioned, their detailing clean and unencumbered by unnecessary accoutrements; even the protruding chimneys are simplified versions of the miniature house forms found in the general area. Both houses are stuccoed masonry

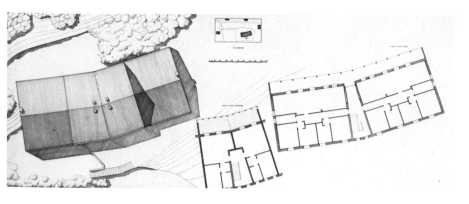

constructions. As is typical of houses in the region, the front and rear façades of the two structures respond to divergent criterion: the front includes a loggia or colonnade, the rear is less articulated. In the case of the larger, three-family house, there is the typical differentiation between the lower and upper loggias: the continuous loggia at ground level has reinforced concrete posts and lintel; above, these posts are continued by timber members. With the single-family house, the gabled ends provide the differentiation. A recessed portico created by four pillars

Casa per tre famiglie, Baiedo
Site and floor plans

Casa unifamiliare, Baiedo
General view from above with the three-family house in the background

and end walls at the ground level indicates the front of the structure. The valley side is more subdued, with a central element of four square windows carefully spaced vertically and horizontally, and two door openings to either side.

In addition, the small piazza in Premana (1984) is further evidence of Luca Scacchetti's subtle use of detail

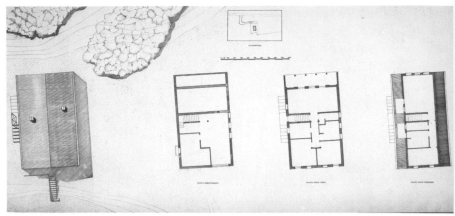

in an irregular space. Here he employs
a house in miniature as the central element of the fountain. He combines
stone and cast-in-place concrete to articulate the same dialogue between old
and new as in his larger constructions.

Casa unifamiliare, Baiedo
Floor plans

Piazza, Premana
View
Elevations and plan

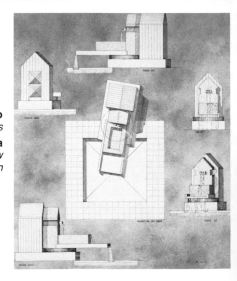

Novara and Surroundings

Convitto Nazionale Carlo Alberto
View of the portico and library building

The city of Novara is an industrial center within an agricultural region. Of Roman origin, its medieval center typically contains a number of arcaded streets retaining their original *castrum* grid. Among these one finds two recent projects by Massimo Fortis, one involving the extension and restructuring of an existing complex, and the other, a new hotel.

The Convitto Nazionale Carlo Alberto is located on the northern edge of the city center. Massimo Fortis designed three new additions to this state boarding school. The first involves the restructuring of the west wing; it includes the cafeteria, classrooms for the secondary school, and rooms for the residents. A bridge building forms the second and contains new library and class spaces. The last is a new structure to house the gymnasium and indoor swimming pool. A new above-ground passage connects the last two. Since the new constructions are within a complex of much older buildings, Massimo Fortis restricted the architectural vocabulary to very simple but elegantly proportioned forms and details. The new additions have concrete structural supports and brick cladding.

On a site immediately south of the cathedral, Fortis' newly built hotel, the Albergo Italia is located adjacent to the excavations of Roman ruins which were left exposed to form a new park. Here, Fortis' solution maintains the integrity of the street edge, while the side to the interior of the block creates a courtyard of archaeological elements. The merit of this project is only in the refined detailing of the exterior elements; the interior of the hotel was not designed by Fortis. Unlike the materials used in the additions to the Convitto, those used in this hotel are much higher in quality. Brick makes way for two kinds of stone veneer—yellow trachyte

Albergo Italia
View along Via Solaroli with the hotel in the center
Detail view from the courtyard

Casa degli anziani
View from the entrance court, still under construction

and Norwegian granite—to differentiate the vertical elements from the infill.

Antonio Monestiroli and his associates have been involved since 1985 in the design of a residential complex for the elderly in Galliate, a small city northeast of Novara. This facility is located on the same square as the community hospital. The structures are arranged to form an elongated double courtyard perpendicular to the street. The peristyle entry court is formed by the commons building and by a companion loggia structure opposite to it. The commons building houses the offices, dining hall, a multipurpose room, and a small apartment for the custodian. A smaller court defined by the two identical residential buildings lies beyond. These buildings are organized with the residents' rooms facing inward, towards the court. The doors for the two buildings terminate the axis of the two colonnades, and in each lobby stairs wrap around the elevator, giving access to the second floor. There is a common sitting area in the middle of the floors, offering the residents a place for activities outside their sleeping rooms. The bathrooms are located at the end of each hallway. Architecturally, the project reflects Monestiroli's training at the Polytechnic in Milan

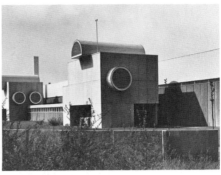

Fattoria Bossi Spa
View of the office building from the road
View of the factory building

and his association with Giorgio Grassi. Its stark architecture, visible in the slender colonnade of the front court, is in fact reminiscent of their student dormitory complex in Chieti. Monestiroli writes:

[Today] it is necessary to again undertake the theoretical debate on design... [each] project...contains three questions that must be addressed: the question of building type, of construction, of form.[15]

Vittorio Gregotti has been designing buildings for Fattoria Bossi Spa in Cámeri since 1956, when the first residential complex for the employees of the textile concern was constructed (a second apartment building dates from 1961). In 1968 and again in 1980,

Vittorio Gregotti and his associates (Lodovico Meneghetti and Giotto Stoppino; Augusto Cagnardi and Pierluigi Cerri) designed facilities for the factory itself. The first was a new manufacturing facility, an interesting structure with cylindrical and semi-cylindrical vents; the second, an extension to the office building. This last project serves as the new entry into the manufacturing complex. It consists of a bullnosed horizontal slab with continuous band windows, decisively modern in its expression, lifted three stories by recessed elements. Display areas, meeting rooms, and administrative offices are housed within. Construction is reinforced concrete, with steel for the roof and its supporting structure.

North of Novara

30.1 Centro sportivo comunale 1984–87
Via Franzi, Borgomanero
Massimo Fortis with Federico Fortis
Public space.

30.2 Pavilione 1973
Outskirts, Borgo Ticino
Aldo Rossi with Giovanni Braghieri
Private.

30.3 Municipio e Piazza Martiri 1981–83
Pombia
Adalberto Caccia, Paolo Colombo, Rita Mangone, Paolo Monti
Visit during regular office hours. The plaza is accessible at all times.

30.4 Cooperativa di abitazione 1980–84
Oleggio
Adalberto Caccia, Paolo Colombo, Rita Mangone, Paolo Monti
The freestanding building is visible from the main highway and is accessible from all sides.

30.5 Residential addition and restoration 1985–86
Via Roma, Oleggio
Paolo Colombo, Rita Mangone, Paolo Monti
The building is across the street from the train station.

Centro sportivo comunale
Site plan

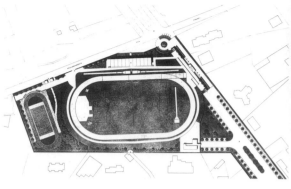

The Ticino River leaves Lake Maggiore in Sesto Calente. The area is partly industrial, partly recreational: the Parco della Valle del Ticino, a national park, straddles the river which forms the border between the regions of Piedmont and Lombardy. Here, the rolling hills give way to the plains. A number of projects, from small pavilions to municipal buildings and town squares, illustrate the best of recent architecture in the Ticino basin.

To the west, in Borgomanero, Massimo Fortis has designed the grandstands and ancillary facilities for the new municipal sports center. He designed this 1984–87 project in association with his father, Federico Fortis. The design of the grandstands differentiates between trussed metal coverture and the reinforced concrete stepped structure of the seating area itself. Below the seats are the changing rooms at ground level and the service facilities at mid level. The elegant roof cantilevers from a dozen support points at the back of the top row of seats, providing an unimpeded view of the playing field. In addition, Fortis designed the entry pavilion and surrounding landscape elements.

A 1973 pavilion by Aldo Rossi is located outside Borgo Ticino. This small structure is on a wooded site overlooking the Ticino River and presents an octastyle portico facing towards the access. The rear elevation is a wall with three windows, the middle one on center. The end walls are plain squares with a central square window and a small, circular attic vent above. The barrel vaulted roof spans between these end walls. Inside there are four rooms including the bathroom. Construction is plastered masonry, with sheet metal roof over wood trusses.

The Milanese firm of Adalberto Caccia, Paolo Colombo, Rita Mangone, and Paolo Monti received the commission to design the municipal building

and adjacent Plaza of the Martyrs in Pombia. This 1981–83 project first establishes a formal and monumental center to this small community, then deals with the particular needs of the municipal offices. Due to the sloping terrain, the building is slightly above the Plaza of the Martyrs. The terraced space is defined on the west side by the stairs leading to the elementary school and by a freestanding peristyle to the east. The south retaining wall is only breached by the steps leading to the entry of the municipal building itself. This compact structure has a slightly elongated plan. The octagonal central area is defined by the perimeter walls of the secondary spaces and the pairs of columns at each corner which support the clerestory and pyramidal roof. This element projects above the rest of the structure, a variation of the massing of Aldo Rossi's school in Fagnano/Olona. From the plaza and the rear, the building appears as two gabled wings with the taller central pavilion. From the west, the façade articulations reinforce the geometry of the plan through the arrangement of the windows and tripartite recessed porticoes of the secondary entries on axis with the central octagon. The east elevation is similarly arranged, but without the recessed porticoes.

Municipio e Piazza Martiri
View from the adjacent school
Interior showing the central space

In Oleggio, there are two projects by Adalberto Caccia, Paolo Colombo, Rita Mangone, and Paolo Monti. The first, a pair of cooperative apartment buildings, were designed and built in 1980–84. The bodies of the buildings are divided into thirds, the center one wider than the flanking two, and, as a result, also taller. The sides have two two-bedroom apartments per floor, the center one has three-bedroom units. Their formal characteristics are rather straight forward, and these connect the design to the traditional farm complexes common to the area. Facing south, the roof overhang is supported

Cooperativa di abitazione
View from the highway exit, the center of town in the background

Residential addition and restoration
View before renovation
View after renovation

by slender, one story columns which rest on somewhat more massive pillars. These protect the continuous balconies. While the upper level seems very open, the lower two floors appear to be exposed only by cutting away large areas from the outermost wall. The north façade, in contrast, is a punched out plane which indicates the central entry point to each one-third. Construction is masonry with a plaster exterior.

The second project by Paolo Colombo, Rita Mangone, and Paolo Monti in Oleggio (Adalberto Caccia having left the firm), across from the train station, is a renovation and addition to a small mixed use building. It dates from 1985–86 and further illustrates their concern for careful detail that maintains a dialogue between existing and new. The addition is minuscule—it involves only slightly over six hundred square feet of new floor area, the living rooms of two apartments. The architects have very elegantly enlarged a rather uninspiring building. The addition occurs in the upper two floors, extending the building towards the corner. What had been an enclosed yard to the corner of the street is cleared and exposed to form an outdoor area for the gelateria in the renovated ground level. Above, the addition is separated from the original structure by small balconies on each level, framed by a pair of columns. These are concrete, as is the wall of the addition, but the structure around the clerestory windows is steel, which further reinforces the differentiation between old and new. Colombo et al. reiterate this by leaving a gap between the steel beam just beyond the inner column and the wall of the original building.

Milano

Gallaratese 2 (Block D)
View from the garden

As the industrial and financial center of Italy, Milan is a city constantly undergoing growth and change. Among the many new structures only a handful stand out, and, not accidentally, they are housing. Much of the new growth has occurred as the postwar construction of bypass roads shifted the new residential areas to the periphery of the nineteenth-century city. Two new residential areas illustrate this expansion. The first, the Gallaratese area to the northwest of the city, dates from the 1970s, while the complex at Vaiano Valle is still under construction. Apartment complexes have also been built along the radial avenues leading away from the city center, and an example is included on Via Graziano Imperatore. Finally, of the various recent infill projects within the historic city, a building on Corso Garibaldi illustrates the integration of current work into the city fabric.

At the Gallaratese complex (1969–74) in northwest Milan, Aldo Rossi's apartment block is the smaller of four buildings of the second section developed in this new residential area; the other three structures are by Carlo Aymonino, who was in charge of the overall planning. Rossi explored a typology of the single-loaded hallway access apartment block. Concerning this, Rossi states:

There is an analogical relationship... that mixes freely with both the corridor typology [and] the architecture of the traditional Milanese tenements, where the corridors signify a life-style bathed in everyday occurrences, domestic intimacy and varied personal relationships.[16]

Stylistically, what results is a low linear building supported by a row of fins on one side and thin piers on the other. These create a ground level colonnade, through which one reaches the five cores leading up to the open-air corridors. A central formal entry is designated by four giant columns—

cylinders which support the end of the longer of two segments of this building. This slab building is small while appearing monumental—it has only two and three floors of apartments. Because of its starkness the design has been criticized as being sterile. Also, it must be stated that Rossi's optimistic assumption that the spaces within the colonnade and along the halls would be enlivened by buzzing activity cannot come to fruition, not so long as there are so few specific public functions at ground level; this is inevitable. The abstract nature of the structure, however, is beginning to show signs of adaptation, as residents add planters to their private terraces or the public passageways. As time passes the harshness will mellow, as the structure adapts more readily to the whims of the residents than even its neighbor by Aymonino.

In the southern part of Milan, a residential complex at Vaiano Valle is formed by a ten-story high-rise transformation of the great rural complexes found in the Lombardian plain. Three groups of architects coordinated design of their respective blocks insofar as building height and perimeter definition are concerned: these standards

Residential complex at Vaiano Valle
General view with Building 1 on the left foreground, Building 3 on the right foreground, and Building 2 in the background.
View of the road between Building 2 on the left and Building 3 on the right

were established by the city planning department. The overall quadrilateral shows a nearly complete perimeter building penetrated by an off-center axis running north-south. In addition to this opening, there is a gap on the northwest corner. Access into the courtyard is gained through each of these

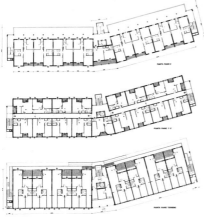

Edilizia residenziale pubblica
Exterior from the road
Floor plans

openings. In reality, the complex is much more like a fortress, especially because of the scale of the blocks and inward focus, the turning away from the chaotic surroundings of this new satellite development.

At ground level and in volume, the buildings are formed by four corner towers which connect to the rest of the volumes above the seventh floor, creating giant portals which are crisscrossed by bridges. In the case of the two segments by Giuseppe Gambirasio and

Giorgio Zenoni (one in association with Giuseppe Grossi and Bruno Minardi), the definition of these portals is clear, since the top floors actually are continuous across each segment, while the brick-clad block by Lorenzo Berni, Aline Leroy, and Alberto Grimoldi appears as two separate segments. The courtyard façade of this block (a dotted-I in plan) is a series of three giant, three-floor horizontal bands articulated by vertical window sections and recessed balconies. The courtyard elevations of the two other segments are more horizontal in design. This is particularly the case in the block designed by Gambirasio and Zenoni alone. Here, the architects alternate color bands every floor of the building. The overall solution is successful, for as Pierluigi Nicolin points out, "[the] Gambirasio-Zenoni team's desire to frame traditional models of mass housing…counterpoints the serene stillness of the Berni-Grimoldi buildings."[17] The block by Berni, Leroy, and Grimoldi received a national prize as the best public housing in 1986.

The apartment building (1980–83) on Via Graziano Imperatore in Milano-Niguarda by Massimo Fortis, Angelo Bugatti, Adalberto Caccia, Paolo

View along Corso Garibaldi

Colombo, Rita Mangone, Paolo Monti, and others is less exotic but clearly a design which resolves the programmatic requirements for public housing in a more subtle way. The two identical six-story structures have a slight bend in the middle, where the elevator cores and primary stairs are located. This helps to define the interior courtyard specified by Fortis as a site for an outdoor market. At ground level, the dwelling units face both ways; in the two levels above, double loaded corridors give access to the apartments; the hallways of the top three floors are single-loaded so units also face both ways. The resulting complex is rich in diversity of apartment types, from one-bedroom units to large, three-bedroom ones. To the courtyard, the lower three floors give the appearance of separate low-rise buildings inserted into a high-rise framework. The outside façades, on the other hand, are like the protective walls around this microcosm of a city.

On Corso Garibaldi near the center of Milan, Luca Scacchetti was asked to design the façade of an infill, nine-story apartment building. Designed in 1984–85, the façade explores a traditional articulation of base, middle, and top typical of structures since the Renaissance. Specifically, Scacchetti alludes to the architecture built in the late nineteenth century, during the post-*Risorgimento* expansion of Milan. He gives the base two elements: one, a rusticated lower two floors with repetitive large openings below a row of small, square perforations; the other, also two stories, which are delineated by two perforated bays with double rows of square windows flanking the four open central bays, and a cornice overhead. Above, the upper five floors are arranged with their central openings delineating a **V**, topped by another row of square openings.

North of Milano

A number of projects of interest are found in the towns to the north of Milan. One is located in Casorezzo and includes an entry pavilion and new office building for the Zucchi industrial concern, designed by Cino Zucchi and Roberto Giussani in 1981–84. The entry pavilion that includes the guard's cabin is a lightweight steel roof supported by six slender concrete columns. The new office building presents quite a contrast. It is a masonry structure and, as such, is basically a heavy solid with small openings. The complex will include a "cash-and-carry" store and warehouse buildings.

Zucchi Industries
Exterior of office building
View of the entry pavilion
Interior view of the new office building

In Nova Milanese Massimo Fortis, Paolo Colombo, and Rita Mangone designed a new public square between 1981 and 1986. This very elegant, sophisticated solution is placed in the middle of a new development. Fortis follows a very traditional approach, completing the fourth side with a combination wall, pergola, and pavilion, all organized about a central axis. The central pavilion alludes to the mythical primitive hut and is roofed with a traditional form lifted at its four corners by small posts. Inside, an amphitheater is formed by the grass slope.

In Gallarate, an industrial city northwest of Milan, four projects by Vittorio Introini illustrate this architect's interest in combining tensile and compressive construction materials in building forms that are archetypical.

Piazza Carlo Fedeli
FIAT automobile dealership

The FIAT dealership is a symmetrical structure with two arms extending to the roadside. The three sides are the automobile showrooms, while the service portion of the structure is to the rear. A perimeter awning is suspended by cables. Below the awning, large window walls are grouped in pairs, separated by very fragile lattice columns which establish the construction module. Above, the cables are attached to the masonry wall on center with small, square clerestory windows. The building is a contrast of light-weight metal elements and solidness of masonry.

In his complex of one- and two-family houses, the "house of the creepers," Introinii makes use of ten-

sion members to create vertical pergolas that cover the structures. The one-family house is placed within a rectangular garden, the lower floor basically an open space with terraces separating the interior spaces from the grass. The living space has a two-level void, with the bedrooms facing toward the garden on either side. The two-family structures are squares with two semi-detached units that are placed within two square gardens.

Two sets of row houses continue this dichotomy. The older of the two, the "house of the tie-rods," is made of five identical units, each with T-shaped floor plans. They are characterized by the use of tension members to support the walkway leading to the front doors. The building is finished in very elegant square tiles and has a flat roof. The row houses are two stories each, somewhat reminiscent of J.J.P. Oud's row houses at the Weissenhof exhibition in Stuttgart, Germany. The second complex, the "house of the temples," presents a contrast. The ends and center houses are narrower, three-story

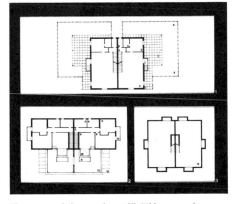

"La casa dei rampicanti" ("House of the creepers")
View of two-family house
Floor plans, two-family house

units, giving the row temple-like gabled fronts at these places. These houses have their stairs against the party walls, and each have four bedrooms. In between each end and the center are four units with the stairs perpendicular to the end walls and located in the center of each house. Aside from their adjacent location, the connection of the newer row of houses to the

139

predecessor is only hinted by the suspended canopy over the entrances.

In contrast to these, Introini's "house of the portals" is located in a mid-block urban site. Introini maintains the street edge with lateral elements that give access along the sides, while the central axis is accentuated by a square building mass elevated above heavy fin walls. The front is a block of three units which forms the carport, and beyond the central walk leads to the rear house. Overall, Introini succeeds in integrating the new project into the urban fabric while permitting privacy within the lot.

Opposite page:
"La casa dei tiranti"
"La casa dei tempio"

This page:
"La casa dei portali"
View along the street
View of the courtyard

Segrate and Vignate

33.1 Piazza del Municipio e monumento ai partigiani 1965
Town center, Segrate
Aldo Rossi
Public square adjacent to the Municipio (town hall).

33.2 Cimitero 1984–86
South edge of town, Vignate
Giancarlo Bentivoglio and Guido Brighi
Open during regular hours every day of the week.

Piazza, Segrate

The towns of Segrate and Vignate, to the east of Milan, are among many in this industrial region experiencing immense growth during the postwar period. Much of this growth has been uninspiring, in the form of typically anonymous blocks of apartment buildings with commercial spaces at ground level in the centers of the towns, with the new industries located along the major highways connecting Milan with Venice to the east and Bologna to the southeast.

In 1965, Aldo Rossi designed the square adjacent to the new town hall in Segrate. The main element of the project is the monument in honor of the partisans who opposed the Fascist regime during the Second World War. Composed of primary forms—a prism, cylinder, slabs, and stepped pyramid—the Segrate monument serves both as a podium and a fountain. The podium at the top of the stepped pyramid faces a terrace at the rear of the plaza. The prism, supported by the cylinder, has an open end from which water falls on a linear shallow basin on the floor of the plaza. As currently executed, Rossi's new town square does not present the complete image as intended. Missing are the free-standing half columns and arcaded wall which would separate the area around the monument from the adjacent city hall and apartment buildings. In its totality, the complex is intended to "construct an architecture of shadows" formed by what appear to be found elements excavated from the site.[18]

The commission for the extension of the cemetery in Vignate was awarded to Giancarlo Bentivoglio and Guido Brighi in 1979. The first segment was completed in 1986. The solution by Bentivoglio and Brighi places the extension to the west of the existing cemetery and encloses the whole

with a new set of columbaria. Its *béton brut* structure, rectilinear and abstract, contrasts with the curvilinear brick walls of the entry. The two-level perimeter structure uses square bays with three rows of three niches each. The lower bays are accessible directly from the open area, while access to the upper level niches is along an open loggia.

Cimitero
View showing the new columbaria
View from the outside

Fagnano/ Olona

34.1 Scuola elementare Salvatore Orrú 1972–76
Via Pasubio, Fagnano/Olona
Aldo Rossi with Giovanni Braghieri
and Arduino Cantafora
Visitors should inquire in the office.

34.2 Casa unifamigliare 1978–83
Via Galileo Galilei / Via Edison,
Fagnano/Olona
Giorgio Grassi
Private.

**Scuola elementare
Salvatore Orrú**
*View of the library from
the courtyard*

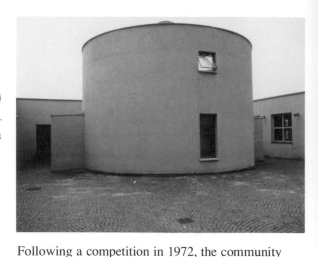

Following a competition in 1972, the community entrusted the construction of its new elementary school to Aldo Rossi. This very enigmatic project has been the subject of strong criticism, particularly because of the imagery and associations attached to its tectonic elements. The composition of the Salvatore Orrú elementary school is based on very simple and elementary components: a central cylindrical volume capped by a transparent conical roof, placed within a rectangular courtyard, from which extend arms containing the classroom spaces. On the side facing the road into town, a pergola leads to a freestanding chimney in front of the central volume of the school. It is the imagery of this latter element that has been the subject of criticism, as it is associated with chimneys of factories (by Rossi) and death camp incinerators (by his detractors). But the project is much more: it is a miniature city, composed of the elements explained by Rossi in *Architecture of the City*.[19] One finds streets, plazas, and monuments transliterated to hallways, courtyard, and central library. The imagery is clear, and the solution fits its programmatic requirements. Classrooms are placed along single loaded corridors, the principal's and nurse's offices are to the front, the gymnasium and common facilities are in the back, adjacent to the athletic fields. The entry is disassociated from the formal organizational axis, since main access is from a side street. A bicycle shed is found to the side of the main walk to the front entrance.

Also in the town is a house by Giorgio Grassi. This single family house of 1978–83 is located in a new residential area. Grassi's architecture, as is the

case with Rossi's, relies on timeless, simple forms, and this structure is no exception. Its rationalist, rather abstract design contrasts with its more typical neighbors. The house is formed by three elements: a portico facing Via Galilei, the volume of the house proper, and a smaller block appended to the back enclosing the bathroom, kitchen, and dining area above the basement garage. Entry is from the cul-de-sac street, Via Edison. The three-bedroom house has a floor area under 1300 square feet.

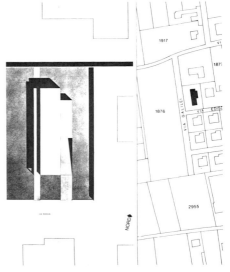

Scuola elementare Salvatore Orrú
View from the entry

Casa unifamigliare
Site plan and location map

Broni

Scuola elementare F. de Amicis
View of the courtyard

The city of Broni is located near the confluence of the Ticino and Po rivers, against the foothills of this wine producing area. It is the site of three projects by Aldo Rossi.

The initial project by Rossi is the 1969–70 renovation and addition to the F. de Amicis elementary school, on the Piazza Italia in the town center. The new intervention consists of a portico entry which faces the common space between school buildings on the site, the central stairs, and service spaces. Two stout corner columns support the thick cornice of the overhang. The new constructions reduced the size of the inside courtyard, which is now defined by an abstract loggia along three sides. The fourth side is a wall which includes a fountain formed by a prism spout over a cubical basin and the rectangular window which lights the stairwell. Behind the loggia, hallways allow access to the classrooms. With this project, Rossi illustrates his belief that, unless one retains the existing structure as is, without the cosmetic replication of the exist-

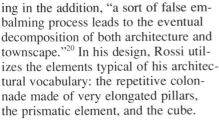

ing in the addition, "a sort of false embalming process leads to the eventual decomposition of both architecture and townscape."[20] In his design, Rossi utilizes the elements typical of his architectural vocabulary: the repetitive colonnade made of very elongated pillars, the prismatic element, and the cube.

The single-family row houses of 1973 offer an alternative to the typical municipal housing. Located in a new residential area to the west of town near the community wine cellars, these three-story houses form a very urban façade to the street. The volume is subdivided by the low elements projecting from the main body of the building. Kitchen, washroom, and storage spaces, together with a carport, are located on the ground level. The main floor houses the living room, master bedroom, and bath, with two additional bedrooms and bath above. Each unit has a garden allotted to the south. The construction is masonry and reinforced concrete, with a painted plaster exterior.

The secondary school is part of a school complex across the street from the row houses. The design and construction date is 1979. The design approach followed by Rossi represents a variation of the composition of the

Case a schiera
Scuola media
View from the approach
View of the auditorium

school in Fagnano/Olona. Here in Broni he forms a quadrilateral to define a courtyard with an object at its center. In the perimeter building the classrooms are arranged facing to the outside. The quadrilateral is crossed by the entry portico and lobby area, from which access is gained to a volume in the center of the court. In this case, it is a theater with entry possible along the axes of symmetry. A gap opposite the entrance pavilion gives access from the courtyard to the activity fields behind the school. The structure is masonry and concrete, stuccoed and painted white, with a standing seam metal roof, painted sky blue.

Province of Bergamo

Case a schiera

There are numerous projects outside of the immediate region of Lombardy that are worthy of mention, either because their design reflects a similar set of concerns, or because they are also designs by the architects surveyed. The projects illustrate the diversity and reach of the design approaches found in the Ticino River Basin. In some cases, they also reflect the traditional rural structures of the particular region. Two examples in the region of Emilia Romagna are a house in Rubiera by Claudio Baldisserri, and an office building by Adolfo Natalini: both are derived from a rural model dating to the eighteenth century by the architect Carlo Francesco Dotti—the same model found in Natalini's bank building in Alzate Brianza near Como.

The area around Bergamo typifies the diversity in topography found in the region. The province of Bergamo has both agricultural and industrial bases, and, in the decades since the end of the Second World War, its smaller towns have undergone growth as the economic fortunes of the major cities have prospered. The city of Bergamo itself is on two sites: the Medieval upper town, on top of a hill, overlooks the new town, a latter foundation located below on relatively flat land. A variety of projects are worth visiting in this province.

In Mapello, west of Bergamo, there is a 1985 group of row houses designed by Mario Cortinovis. The units are arranged in two buildings of six dwellings each. The houses themselves are two story structures, placed with similar functions adjacent to the common walls: stairs and services against stairs and services, and living rooms against living rooms, for example. The design by Cortinovis reflects his appreciation for and understanding of the traditional rural structures found in the area. The buildings are very simple, gabled structures, constructed of masonry and reinforced concrete. The exterior is painted

stucco, with green painted wood window and door frames and tile roofing.

Nearby, a similar solution is found in the four row houses by Aldo Rossi. Located in the suburban town of Mozzo, just outside Bergamo, these 1977 units are identical two-story houses placed perpendicular to the road. The entrance to each, up a short flight of stairs, leads to the main floor of each unit. Their plan is very simple, with a large room to either side of the entry hall. Stairs lead to the upper floor, which has three bedrooms and the bathroom. Below the main floor is a basement with garage and a service area. Each of the units opens to the south; balconies on both floors give this façade the appearance of a continuous loggia.

The new terminal and office building for the regional bus line T.B.S.O. is located between the communities of Osio Sotto and Boltiere. The structure by Massimo Fortis, dating from 1983–85, includes a public area with waiting spaces, ticket office, and cafeteria on the ground level with the various offices above. A space frame provides overall coverture to the building and is supported by slender steel columns; nearly half of its span cantilevers beyond the structure as a canopy over the bus berths. Inserted below is an elegantly symmetrical concrete masonry building, its center third of glass extending across the top of the wall as a continuous band.

Case unifamiliare
View of the rear of the houses
View from the street

Sede Autolinee T.B.S.O.
Interior view

Sede Autolinee T.B.S.O.
Cooperativa d'abitazione
View from the west
View from the plaza

Mario Cortinovis is the architect of a cooperative apartment building in Seriate. This six-story building, its first phase completed in 1980–82, has elements reminiscent of Adolf Loos's Michaelerplatz building in Vienna. Cortinovis has designed an urban structure that mediates between city and countryside in a clearer manner than its neighbors. On the west side, there is a portal projecting from the center pavilion of the building. One can see through a total of six structural bays, with the center two combined into a tall opening connecting the two sides. The slab has a continuous colonnade along the wall that faces the plaza to the east. The body of the building is pink while the colonnade is green. The apartment units themselves are reached by way of open corridors, screened by the regularly perforated exterior wall. All are based on the repetitive module established by the structural bays.

Province of Mantova

37.1 Cooperativa d'abitazione 1979
Via Pedagno, Goito
Aldo Rossi (with Gianni Bragheri and COPRAT)
Private.

37.2 Cooperativa d'abitazione 1979
Via Albert Einstein, Pegognana
Aldo Rossi (with Gianni Bragheri and COPRAT)
Private.

Cooperativa d'abitazione, Goito
View within the courtyard
General view

Aldo Rossi has realized two housing complexes in towns near the city of Mantova (or Mantua), in the province of the same name. Both projects, located in new subdivisions within small towns, were built with the COPRAT cooperative and share a similar formal concern for the expression of house as an archetypal object within a communal context. In the case of the 1979 complex in Goito, Rossi has designed the party wall dwelling units with attached garages so as to permit the two-story, two-family houses to be seen as separate objects. Little house-like entry elements protrude into the cul-de-sac street to further differentiate the units, with the entries to the adjacent houses on opposite sides, thus giving each a private entrance. The parallel rows of houses are constructed using traditional techniques, finished in stucco with painted metal roofs.

The second housing complex is located in Pegognana, to the south of Mantova. Also dating from 1979, it presents a contrasting solution. In this case, the two parallel buildings face each other through a

high portico. Their architecture is reminiscent of traditional Lombardian farm complexes, where a common roof supported by simple columns covers rooms housing the various agricultural functions. A one-story garage and entry building closes the common space from the street.

Cooperativa d'abitazione, Pegognana
Detail view
Exterior

Province of Módena

38.1 Cimitero S. Cataldo 1971–87
Módena
Aldo Rossi (with Gianni Braghieri)
Sections are still under construc-
tion; the cemetery is open seven
days a week.

Cimitero S. Cataldo
View of the ossuary

The 1971 competition for the extension of the
cemetery of San Cataldo in Módena was won by
Aldo Rossi with G. Braghieri. Their project
proposed to extend the neoclassical cemetery with a
new section to the west. In concept, the new
cemetery reflects the dimensional definition of the
earlier cemetery. It incorporates the Jewish
cemetery, built outside the walls of the 1858 complex, since in the new complex it becomes the pivo-
tal element of the overall composition. In Rossi's
project, the surrounding structure and a row of trees
enclose the new cemetery space with as equal
rigidity as the original. The architectonic expression
of the new "house of death,"[21] however, is less
opulent, almost barren, for in Rossi's methodology
the architecture should be devoid of any references
to time—based on archetypal forms that he explains
in *The Architecture of the City*.[22] The new complex
is defined by an external C-shaped and gabled building with three floors of wall burial cells. A two
floor, flat roofed columbarium is placed within this.
On the center axis and between these two buildings
is the cubic roofless house, an ossuary whose image
is an unfinished house—or is it a house without its
roof, a house ruin?—and speaks about the fragile
and transitory nature of life. Other elements of the
Rossi project include the loggia building parallel to
the perimeter structure which faces the Jewish and
old cemeteries and the perpendicular building housing the chapels. Since the beginning of construction,
the rather stark buildings have begun to mellow as

153

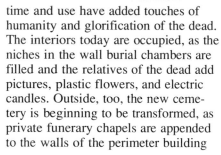

time and use have added touches of humanity and glorification of the dead. The interiors today are occupied, as the niches in the wall burial chambers are filled and the relatives of the dead add pictures, plastic flowers, and electric candles. Outside, too, the new cemetery is beginning to be transformed, as private funerary chapels are appended to the walls of the perimeter building

Cimitero S. Cataldo
*View of the arcade building (left) and the perimeter building (right)
Interior view of the top floor, perimeter building*

where it faces the loggia and the old cemetery. Meanwhile, construction continues towards the completion of the new complex.

Province of Réggio Emilia

39.1 Conzorsio del Fromaggio Parmigiano Reggiano 1978–83
Via Emilia Oveste and Via L. Cervi, Réggio nell' Emilia
Guido Canali
Can be visited during regular office hours.

39.2 Villa Molinari 1980–83
Viale Maria Melato, 12, Rubiera
Claudio Baldisserri
Private.

Two projects in the province of Réggio Emilia present contrasting responses to regional antecedents. A very abstract interpretation results in the headquarters for the consortium of cheese producers of Parma and surrounding areas. The structure by Guido Canali (1978–83) is located to the north of Réggio, on the ancient via Emilia leading to Parma. Built in prefabricated concrete and concrete block, the building consists of a series of parallel zones. Two are trabeated structures of prefabricated elements, one is a narrow linear solid, a fourth is a glasshouse, and the fifth is an open space. These parallel zones are arranged to formalize the entry into what in reality is a laboratory and office building, but which must also serve as the symbol for the cheese producers. Access from the east and west is along a ramp raising between a skeletal trabeated structure. An off-center perpendicular bridge crosses

Conzorsio del Fromaggio Parmigiano Reggiano

Villa Molinari
Axonometric view showing the interior

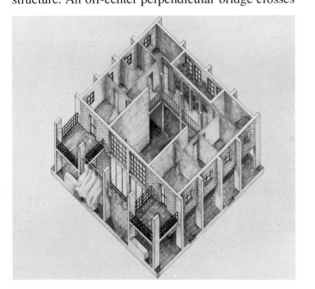

the open space and leads to the second post-and-lintel zone. The functional organization within the building occurs on opposite sides of a central spine housed under the greenhouse. On the axial center of the building is the auditorium, occupying its full width, with the other primary spaces placed to either side within the filled-in trabeated structure. The offices are to the west of the entry lobby on three floors, the auditorium faces to the east, and the laboratories at the end face west.

In contrast, the Molinari House (1983), located in a suburban area to the south of Rubiera, is a contemporary interpretation of traditional building typologies found in the region of Emilia Romagna. Beginning with the traditional building type found throughout the region—based on Dotti's model hay loft—Claudio Baldisserri develops a house that functions like a Roman atrium house, with the

Villa Molinari
Interior
View from the Viale Maria Melato

central double volume of the living room serving as the organizing space around which the other spaces of the house are placed. The great hip roof appears to hover over the house volume from the outside, its spidery, fin-like columns lifting roof and upper floor as they inscribe a square ground plane. The structure is of reinforced concrete with modular masonry infill walls, and painted wood window and door frames.

Province of Bologna

40.1 Centro elettocontabile, Negozio D&C 1979–81
Via Nannetti / Via Piemonte / Via Roma, Zola Predrosa
Adolfo Natalini and Roberto Magris
The computer center cannot be visited; it is visible from Via Roma and Via Piemonte.

Centro elettocontabile, Negozio D&C
View from the road

In the industrial outskirts of Bologna, the new computer center for the import and export firm D&C resulted from a similar understanding of regional architecture as the work in the Ticino River Basin. In discussing the design for the computer center, Adolfo Natalini refers to Dotti and his model hay loft, the prevalent agricultural structure in the region:

Carlo Francesco Dotti's eighteenth century model... marked and still marks the Bolognese plain with a series of works of architecture.... Our building with its links to this tradition shows how architecture can contain machines (but not vice versa), that traditional techniques can live happily with the most sophisticated... that history serves to give hope for the future.[23]

This concept of a roof supported by a series of perimeter columns underlies the design of the new structure. The roof of the elongated parallelogram of the D&C computer center is supported by flat pillars in brick and prefabricated concrete elements. Under this superstructure, the various functions occur on three floors, with the computer equipment located in the lower floor, offices and other spaces above.

archetype: The original or first example which embodies the most fundamental characteristics; it is applied by analogical extension in architecture, especially by Neo-Rationalists, including those part of the *Tendenza*.

atrium: The inner court in Roman domestic architecture, open to the sky; in current usage, it also refers to an enclosed space, usually surrounded by a colonnade and around which are arranged the functional spaces of a building.

béton brut: French term used to describe concrete left exposed or in the raw.

Borromini, Francesco: (1599–1667) The most original of the Baroque architects in Rome, rival and contemporary of Bernini. His best known works are the church of S. Carlo alle Quattro Fontane and S. Ivo della Sapienza, both in Rome. Born in Bissone on Lake Lugano, his portrait adorns the new 100 Swiss Franc notes.

brise-soleil: Refers to a sun-screen or louvers, arranged vertically or horizontally across the façade of a building so as to control its exposure to the sun.

Brutalism: (Also, New Brutalism) The term was coined in England in the early 1960s to identify architecture of the 1950s and 1960s built primarily of reinforced concrete where the material is left exposed (see *béton brut*).

camera obscura: Latin meaning "dark chamber"; used to describe the technical principle behind the photographic camera: a darkened chamber with a minute opening through which an image is received and focused, inverted, onto a receiving surface.

casa a ringhiera: Italian term for a house forming a ring and enclosing an atrium or courtyard, of much smaller scale than the great *cascine* or farm complexes found in the Piemontese and Lombardian plains.

cascine: A farm or agricultural complex, in Italian.

castrum: The archetypal Roman military camp found throughout the empire; it is laid out as a rectangle with the two intersecting axis (the *cardo* and *decumanus*) ending at four gates. Many cities in northern Italy and the rest of Europe dating to Roman times began as such settlements.

columbarium: (plural, columbria) The wall or vault with niches where urns with the ashes of the dead are placed.

"domino frame": A framing system developed by Le Corbusier consisting of posts or columns supporting a floor or roof slab, all constructed in reinforced concrete.

Dotti, Carlo Francesco: (c. 1670–1759) Late Baroque architect from Bologna.

Fontana, Domenico: (1543–1607) Born near Lugano, was architect to Sixtus V; began the layout of Baroque Rome, including the radiating street pattern from S. Maria Maggiore and the placement of the obelisk in S. Peter's square. His works include the Lateran Palace in Rome and the Vatican Library.

frontispiece: Usually refers to the entry bay of a building, though it also refers to the main façade.

grotto: In the Swiss canton of Ticino, refers to a cave-like place, usually used for store but also serving as an eatery or tavern.

hexastyle: Refers to a portico with six frontal columns.

impluvium: The cistern or receptacle that collects rainwater in the middle of the atrium of a Roman house; also used to refer to the uncovered space in the atrium.

in antis: A portico with its columns between end walls, as opposed to a prostyle portico, where the columns stand in front of the body of the building.

Le Corbusier: (1887–1966) Most influential French architect, born in La Chaux-de-Fonds, Switzerland. The impact of his works and writings make him the preeminent architect of the twentieth century. (See *The Le Corbusier Guide*)

loggia: A gallery which opens to one or more sides, usually as part of a building, though also free-standing, and usually arcaded or colonnaded.

Maderno, Carlo: (1556–1629) Italian Renaissance architect, born at Capolago on Lake Lugano. Nephew of Domenico Fontana, he was appointed architect of S. Peter's in 1603, to which he added the nave and façade.

Neo-Rationalism: (See *Tendenza*)

Neoclassicism: The period of the Enlightenment, when a classical architecture was reinterpreted in response to the prevalent Late Baroque; specifically, architecture of the late 17th century to the early 18th century.

nine-square: A common organization for buildings of varying scales; an archetypal Palladian plan, such as found in his Villa Capra, with a center space around which all spaces are organized. The organization varies from that of an atrium plan in that its center space is usually the primary one.

octastyle: Term used to describe a portico with eight columns along the front.

pergola: Enclosure over a walk, formed by columns and beams, usually covered with climbing plants.

peristyle: A row of columns which surround a building or court.

piano nobile: The "noble level" or main floor of a house, usually raised one story above ground by a base housing support spaces.

pilotis: Pillars or stilts, in French, used to raise a building above the ground. Most of Le Corbusier's works are raised above the ground in this manner.

posts and lintels: Vertical and horizontal structural elements.

quoins: Dressed stones which highlight the corners of buildings.

Risorgimento: Literally, resurgence or resurrection, in Italian; the period leading to Italian re-unification after centuries of city-states, foreign occupations, and small kingdoms.

Rogers, Ernesto: (1909–69) Important Italian architect, partner of the firm BBPR and one of the Italian rationalists of the 1930s active in the debates of the CIAM (International Congress of Modern Architects); editor first of the journal *Domus* and then *Casabella-continuità* and professor in the Faculty of Architecture in Milan, he was mentor to the generation of young architects of the postwar period, including Vittorio Gregotti, who succeeded him as editor of *Casabella*.

rotonda: (English: rotunda) A circular room or building, usually with a dome.

rustico: (plural: rustici) Literally, a farmhouse; used to refer to any rural or rustic structure.

Scarpa, Carlo: (1902–78) Long-time teacher at the University Institute of Architecture in Venice and an early proponent of the new architecture of the Modern Movement, his post-war buildings are more and more concerned with how materials are placed, in particular where inserted within historic structures while remaining true to the tenets of the Modern Movement.

Serliana: (also known as Palladian motif)

Sforza: Family name of the Dukes of Milan, who ruled what is now the Canton of Ticino, Lombardy, and Piedmont.

Stam, Mart: (1899–1986) Dutch architect and active participant in the CIAM, of which he was one of the founding members. He was one of the architects of the Weissenhofsiedlung in Stuttgart, worked in Frankfurt on social housing, taught at the Bauhaus in Dessau, and worked in the USSR in the early 1930s. An ardent socialist, he taught in the German Democratic Republic from 1948 to 1952. Thereafter he practiced in Amsterdam.

Tendenza: The Neo-Rationalists, Swiss and Italian, included in this *Guide*.

Terragni, Giuseppe: (1904–43) Born near Milan, he studied at the Polytechnic. Terragni formed the Gruppo 7 with six classmates and became the best known of the Italian rationalists of the 1930s. His Casa del Fascio in Como is possibly the most important monument of the movement.

Tessenov, Heinrich: (1876–1950) German architect and proponent of the Arts and Crafts movement in Weimar Germany.

trabeated: Descriptive adjectives for buildings constructed with post-and-lintel frames.

Weissenhofsiedlung: 1927 housing exposition sponsored by the German Werkbund. The participating architects included Ludwig Mies van der Rohe—who created the master plan and one of the structures—Le Corbusier, J.J.P. Oud, Mart Stam, and others, all seminal members of the Modern Movement.

Woods, Shadrach: (1923–73) American architect who worked with Le Corbusier after the Second World War; formed Candilis-Josic-Woods with two other former associates. His design for the Free University in Berlin (1969) is based on a tartan grid that fixes circulation spaces and leaves the spaces within to be divided according to need, whether it be lecture halls, laboratories, or offices.

General and specific works on the autochthonous architecture of the region

BIBLIOGRAPHY

Switzerland

Amsler, Thomas, Dieter Herrmann, Knut Lohrer, and Ulfert Weber. *Corippo: Bauaufnahme an der TH Stuttgart 1959.* Stuttgart: Karl Kramer Verlag, 1986.

Bukowski, Manfred, Roland Dorn, Bernd Lohse, and Cord Machens. *Tessin: Bergdörfer und Neue Villen.* 8th ed. Braunschweig: Technischen Universität Braunschweig, 1981.

Gschwend, Max. *La casa rurale nel Canton Ticino.* 2 vols. Basel: Verlag G. Krebs AG, 1982.

Rossi, Aldo, Eraldo Consolascio, and Max Bosshard. *La costruzione del territorio: Uno studio sul Canton Ticino.* Milan: CLUP, 1985. Abridged version of *La costruzione del territorio nel Cantone Ticino.* Vol. 1, *Costruzione del territorio e spazio urbano nel Cantone Ticino.* Lugano: Fondazione Ticino Nostro, 1979.

Italy

Barbieri, Giuseppe, and Lucio Gambi, eds. *La casa rurale in Italia.* Florence: Leo S. Olschki Editore, 1970; reprint, 1982.

Castellano, Aldo. *La casa rurale in Italia.* Milan: Edizioni Electa, 1986.

Guidoni, Enrico, ed. *L'architettura popolare in Italia. Rome/Bari: Editori Laterza.*

Nangeroni, Giuseppe, and Roberto Pracchi. *La casa rurale nella montagna lombarda.* 2 vols. Florence: Leo S. Olschki Editore, 1957, 1958.

Nice, Bruno, Gino Pratello, Giuseppe Barbieri, and Elvira Boriani. *La casa rurale nell'Appennino emiliano e nell'Oltrepo pavese.* Florence: Leo S. Olschki Editore, 1953.

Saibene, Cesare. *La casa rurale nella pianura e nella collina lombarda.* Florence: Leo S. Olschki Editore, 1955; reprint, 1980.

General works on contemporary architecture in the region

Switzerland

Blaser, Werner. *Architecture 70/80 in Switzerland.* Basel: Birkhäuser Verlag, 1981.

Disch, Peter. *50 anni di architettura in Ticino 1930–1980 (Quaderno della Rivista Tecnica della Svizzera italiana).* Bellinzona-Lugano: Grassico Pubblicità SA, 1983.

Fumagalli, Paolo, and Attilio Panzeri eds. *BSK Architettura in Ticino: Architektur im Tessin: Architecture au Tessin.* [Lugano?]: Edizioni A. Salvioni & Co., [1987?]

Rastorfer, Darl. "Architects of the Ticino." *Architectural Record* 175, no. 4 (April 1987): 110–27.

Tendenzen: Neuer Architektur im Tessin (exhibition catalogue). Zurich: ETH, 1975.

Italy

Bofanti, Ezio, Rosaldo Bonicalzi, Aldo Rossi, Massimo Scolari, and Daniele Vitale. *Architettura Razionale*. Milan: Franco Angeli Editore, 1973. [*Arquitectura racional*. Madrid: Alianza Editorial, 1979]

Casciato, Maristella, and Giorgio Muratore, eds. *Annali dell' - Architettura Italiana Contemporanea 1984*. Rome: Officina Edizioni, 1985.

Morton, David. "Tendenza." *Progressive Architecture* 61, no. 10 (October 1984): 49–65.

Nicolin, Pierluigi. "Castles in the Plain; Housing on the Periphery." *Lotus International*, no. 48/49 (4/1985–1/1986): 176–89.

Portoghesi, Paolo. *I nuovi architetti italiani*. Rome/Bari: Editori Laterza, 1985.

Monographs and other sources on the works of specific architects

Mario Botta

Battisti, Emilio, and Kenneth Frampton. *Mario Botta: Architecture and Projects in the '70*. Milan: Electa Editrice, 1979.

Battisti, Emilio. "The Intelligence of Architecture as Craft: Works by Mario Botta." *Lotus International*, no. 22 (1/1979): 60–68.

Carloni, Tita. "Architect of the Wall and not of the Trilith: Building and Mario Botta." *Lotus International*, no. 37 (1/1983): 34–46.

Dal Co, Francesco. *Mario Botta: Architecture 1960–1985*. Paris: Electa Moniteur; New York: Rizzoli International, 1986.

Frampton, Kenneth. "Botta's Paradigm" *Progessive Architecture* 65, no. 12 (December 1984): 82–90.

Gilardoni, Virgilio. "Gli spazi dell'uomo nell'architettura di Mario Botta." *Archivio Storico Ticinese*, no. 100 (December 1984): 219–24.

Miller, Nori, and Livio Dimitriu. "Transfigurer of Geometry." *Progressive Architecture* 63, no. 7 (July 1982): 54–63.

Nicolin, Pierluigi, and François Chaslin. *Mario Botta 1978–1982*. Milan: Electa Editrice, 1983.

Purini, Franco. "Inner Voices: Observations on Architecture and Mario Botta." *Lotus International*, no. 48/49 (4/1985–1/1986): 67–93.

Stein, Karen D. "A Tree Grows in Lugano. *Architectural Record* 174, no. 8 (July 1986): 132–37.

Trevisiol, Robert. *La casa rotonda*. Milan: Edizione L'Erba Voglio, 1982.

Mario Campi, Franco Pesina, and Niki Piazzoli

Frampton, Kenneth. "In the Lugano Landscape: Five Architectures." *Casabella* 534, vol 51 (April 1987): 4–11.

Seligmann, Werner, and Jorge Silvetti. *Mario Campi and Franco Pessina*. New York: Rizzoli International, 1987.

"The Mountain and the Machine." *Progressive Architecture* 63, no. 7 (July 1982): 64–71.

"Within the Bounds of Reason." *Architectural Record* 174, no. 8 (July 1986): 88–91.

Guido Canali

Morton, David. "Cheese Biz." *Progressive Architecture* 65, no. 7 (July 1984): 92–98.

Giancarlo Durisch

Durisch, Giancarlo. "Analogous Figures." *Lotus International*, no. 15 (June 1977): 122–27.

Massimo Fortis

"Reseña de proyectos." *Arquitectura* (Madrid) no. 215 (November–December 1978): 22–23.

Aurelio Galfetti

"Castelgrande e Bellinzona." *Abitare*, no. 252 (March 1987): 164–73.

"In the City and on the Crag: Two Projects by Aurelio Galfetti for Bellinzona." *Lotus International*, no. 48/49 (4/1985–1/1986): 94–117.

Giorgio Grassi

"Giorgio Grassi" (issue). *2c: Construcción de la Ciudad*, no. 10 (December 1977).

Moschini, Francesco. *Giorgio Grassi: Progetti 1960–1980*. Florence: Centro Di, 1984.

Vittorio Gregotti
Tafuri, Manfredo. *Vittorio Gregotti*. New York: Electa/Rizzoli, 1982.

Rudy Hunziker
Hofmann, Rinaldo, ed. *Case da vendere—Ready Houses*. Mendrisio: Associazione Culturale SPAZIOARTE, 1983, 51–67.
Rudy Hunziker. Old Westbury, N.Y.: New York Institute of Technology, 1986.

Giancarlo Motta and Antonia Pizzigoni
Motta, Giancarlo, and Antonia Pizzigoni. *La Casa e la città*. Milan:CLUP, 1987.

Adolfo Natalini
Natalini, Adolfo. *Figures of Stone*. (Lotus Documents 3). New York: Rizzoli International, 1984.
Natalini, Adolfo. "Stone-Clad Building: Premises of the Cassa Rurale e Artigiana in Alzate Brianza, Como." *Lotus International*, no. 40 (4/1983): 4–19.
Natalini, Adolfo. "Two-Way Building: Traditional Container and Sophisticated Content." *Lotus International*, no. 37 (1/1983): 52–60.
Savi, Vittorio. "Story of a Design: Adolfo Natalini and One of his Works." *Lotus International*, no. 40 (4/1983): 19–21.

Bruno Reichlin and Fabio Reinhart
Nicolin, Pierluigi. "Intrinsic Architecture: Works by Bruno Reichlin and Fabio Reinhart." *Lotus International*, no. 22 (1/1979): 94–106.

Aldo Rossi
Abercrombie, Stanley. "Italy: The First Built Part of a Cemetery Famous before Building Began." *Architecture (AIA Journal)* 72, no. 8 (August 1983): 162–67.
Arnell, Peter, and Ted Bickford, eds. *Aldo Rossi: Buildings and Projects*. New York: Rizzoli International, 1985.
Braghieri, Gianni. *Aldo Rossi*. Barcelona: Editorial Gustavo Gili, S.A., 1981.
Moschini, Francesco, ed. *Aldo Rossi: Projects and Drawings 1962–1979*. Florence: Cemtro Di, 1979.
Rossi, Aldo. *Three Cities: Perugia, Milano, Mantova* (Lotus Documents 4). New York: Rizzoli International, 1984.
Savi, Vittorio. "Aldo Rossi." *Lotus International*, no. 11 (1/1976): 42–56.
Savi, Vittorio. *L'architettura di Aldo Rossi*. Milan: Franco Angeli Editore, 1976.

Luca Scacchetti
Moschini, Francesco, ed. *Luca Scacchetti: Forme, Oggetti, Architetture 1975–1985*. Rome: Edizioni Kappa, 1986.

Luigi Snozzi
Croset, Pierre-Alain. "Three Buildings for Monte Carasso." *Casabella* 506, vol. 48 (October 1984): 52–63.
Jehle-Schulte Strathaus, Ulrike, Kenneth Frampton, and Vittorio Gregotti. *Luigi Snozzi*. Milan: Electa Editrice, 1984.
Luigi Snozzi: Urban Renewal at Monte Carasso (exhibition catalogue). London: 9H Gallery, 1986.

Livio Vacchini
Bonell, Esteve. "Escola al Ticino." *Quaderns d'arquitectura i urbanisme*, no. 160 (January/February/March, 1984): 86–97.
Norberg-Schulz, Christian, and J.C. Vigato (introductions). *Livio Vacchini*. Barcelona: Gustavo Gili Editores, 1987.

1. Aurelio Galfetti, "In the City and on the Crag: Restoration of Castelgrande in Bellinzona," *Lotus International*, no. 48/49 (4/1985–1/1986): 111.

2. *Luigi Snozzi: Urban Renewal at Monte Carasso*, exhibition catalogue (London: 9H Gallery, 1986): 5.

3. On a low retaining wall facing the town center, an inscription proclaims "Premio Beton 85."

4. *Luigi Snozzi: Urban Renewal*, 4.

5. Livio Vacchini, "Ricostruzione a Vogorno," *Rivista Technica*, no. 7–8 (1986): 28.

6. Aldo Rossi, Eraldo Consolascio, and Max Bosshard, *La costruzione del territorio: Uno studio sul Canton Ticino* (Milan: CLUP, 1985): 136–41.

7. *Luigi Snozzi: Urban Renewal*, 4.

8. "Casa con riscladamento solare a Bigorio," *Rivista Tecnica della Svizzera italiana*, no. 8 (August 1980): 12.

9. Werner Seligmann, "The Poetics of Counterpoint," in *Mario Campi-Franco Pessina Architects* (New York: Rizzoli International, 1987), 11.

10. "Critique," *Progressive Architecture* 63, no. 7 (July 1982): 71.

11. Seligmann, *Mario Campi-Franco Pessina Architects*, 93.

12. Kenneth Frampton, "Un delicato palladianesimo," *Casabella*, no. 534 (April 1987): 7.

13. Quoted in *Quaderns d'arquitectura i urbanisme*, no. 160 (January–March 1984): 88.

14. Adolfo Natalini, "Stone-Clad Building," *Lotus International*, no. 40 (4/1983): 5.

15. Quoted in Paolo Portoghesi, *I nuovi architetti italiani* (Rome/Bari: Editori Laterza, 1985), 363.

16. Quoted by Kenneth Frampton in *Modern Architecture: A Critical History* (London: Thames & Hudson, 1980), 291.

17. Pierluigi Nicolin, "Castles on the Plain," *Lotus International*, no. 48–49 (4/1985–1/1986): 180.

18. *Aldo Rossi: Buildings and Projects* (New York: Rizzoli International, 1985), 53.

19. Aldo Rossi, *L'architettura della città* (Padova: Marsilio Editori, 1966). English translation: *The Architecture of the City* (Cambridge, Mass.: The MIT Press, 1982).

20. *Aldo Rossi: Buildings and Projects*, 85.

21. *A Scientific Autobiography*, 55. See Rafael Moneo's discussion of Rossi's cemetery project, "Aldo Rossi: The Idea of Architecture and the Modern Cemetery," *Oppositions* 5 (1976): 1–30.

22. Cambridge, Mass.: The MIT Press, 1982.

23. "Looking at History," *Domus*, no. 633 (November 1982): 16.

MAPS

Bellinzona and Carasso
pp. 31–37

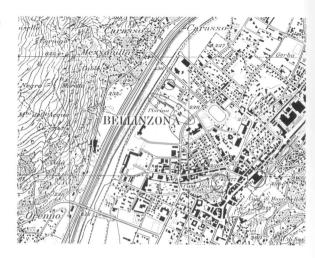

Camorino pp. 42–43

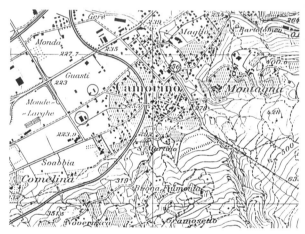

Locarno pp. 50–52

Ascona and Losone pp.
56–58

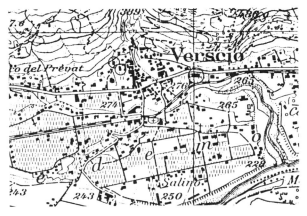

Verscio pp. 59–62

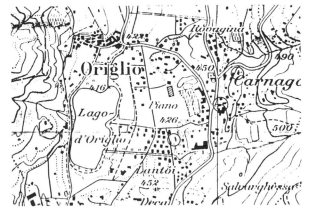

Origlio pp. 66–68

Tesserete, Bigorio,
Cagiallo and Vaglio pp.
69–73

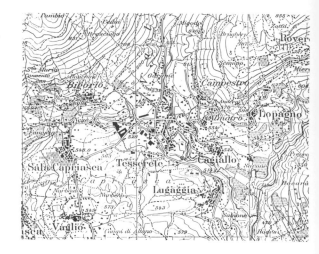

Sonvico and Cadro pp.
74–77

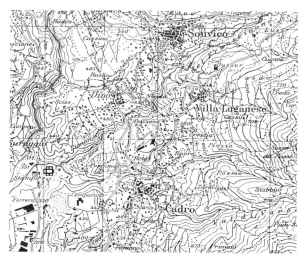

Arosio pp. 78–80

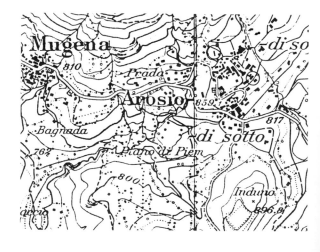

Cureglia pp. 81–83

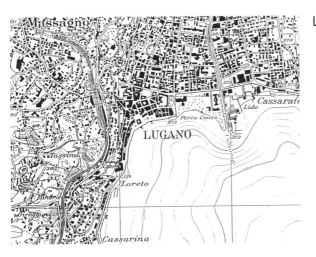

Lugano pp. 84–87

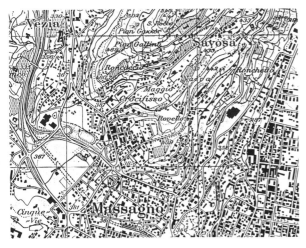

Massagno and Porza
pp. 88–91

Pregassona and
Viganello pp. 92–94

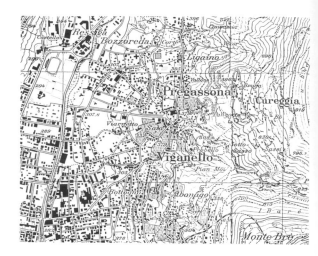

Muzzano, Breganzona
and Sorengo pp. 95–97

Caslano and Neggio
pp. 100–102

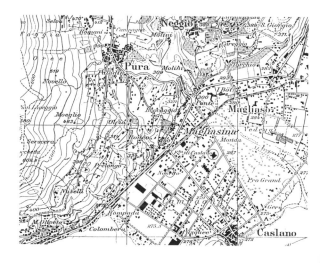

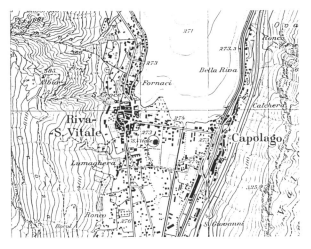

Riva San Vitale pp. 103–106

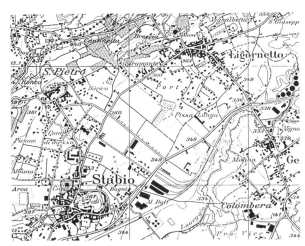

Ligornetto, Stabio and San Pietro/Stabio pp. 107–111

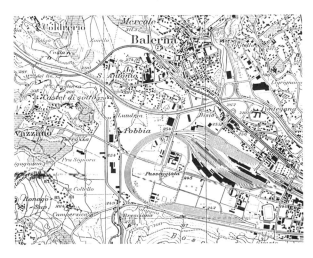

Balerna pp. 112–18

Castel San Pietro, Morbio Superiore and Inferiore pp. 112–18

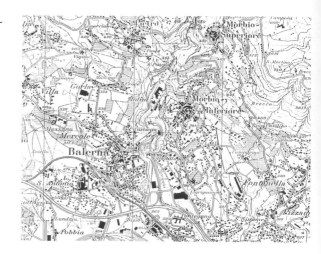

North of Chiasso: Vacallo pp. 119–21

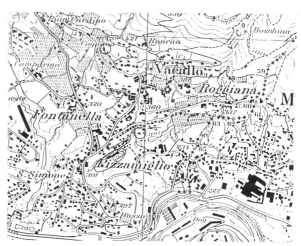

South of Como: Alzate Brianza and Sirone pp. 122–23

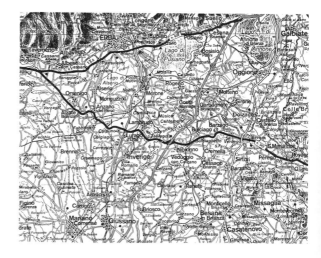

Novara pp. 127–29

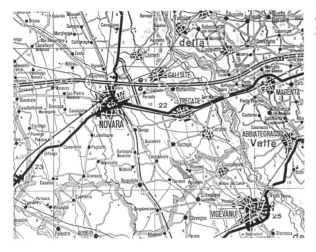

Around Novara pp. 127–29

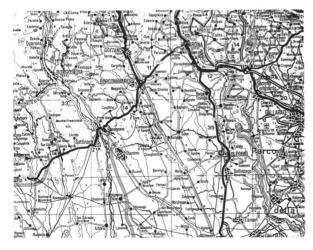

North of Novara pp. 130–32

Casorezzo pp. 137–41

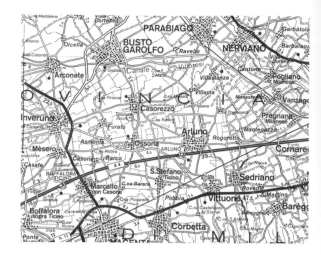

Gallarate pp. 137–41

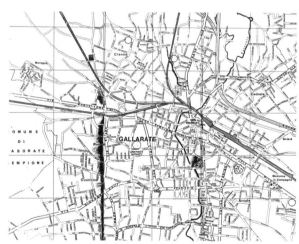

Fagnano/Olona pp.
144–45

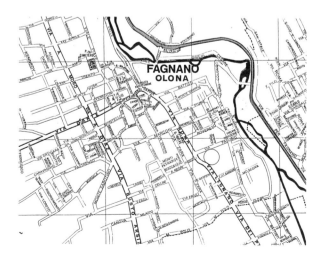

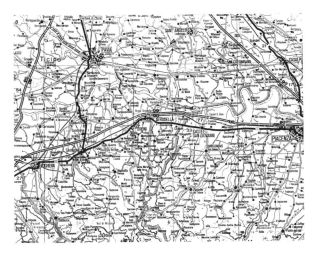

Broni pp. 146–47

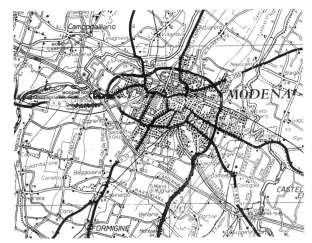

Módena pp. 153–54

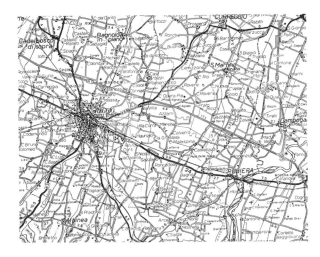

Province of Réggio
Emilia pp. 155–56

INDEX

Born in Mexico, D.F. in 1949, Gerardo Brown-Manrique emigrated with his family to upstate New York in 1962. He pursued undergraduate professional studies at Rensselaer Polytechnic Institute, and received his master of architecture degree from Cornell University in 1974. Brown-Manrique is a professor of architecture at Miami University in Oxford, Ohio, where he has taught since 1978. He is a registered architect in Oklahoma and Ohio and is certified by the NCARB. Included among his writings are the introduction to *O.M. Ungers:Works in Progress 1976–1980* titled "Morphologies, Transformations and Other Stories: Recent Work by O.M. Ungers" (Rizzoli, 1981), as well as the essays "Schloss Morsborich: Ungers' Museum Project in Leverkusen" (*Architectural Design*, 50:1/2, 1980), "Konstantinplatz in Trier: Between Memory and Place" (*Places*, 3:1, 1986), and "The White House" (*Progressive Architecture*, 63:10, 1982).

Brown-Manrique was a National Endowment for the Humanities Summer Fellowship recipient in 1977, and a Fulbright Lecturer to Argentina in 1988.